Styletini

SHAKE UP YOUR STYLE
STIR UP YOUR CONFIDENCE

By: Ashley Martini, MBA, Style Consultant

BROOKLINE PRESS, LLC

www.BrooklinePress.com

Info@BrooklinePress.com

© 2014 Brookline Press, LLC

Published by Brookline Press, LLC

800 Fairway Drive, Suite 340

Deerfield Beach, Florida 33441

Telephone: 561-953-1322

Fax: 561-953-1940

E-mail: Info@BrooklinePress.com

Website: www.BrooklinePress.com

This book is designed to provide accurate and authoritative information on the subject of Fashion. It is sold with the understanding that neither the author nor the publisher is engaged in rendering legal, accounting, or other professional advice. As each individual situation is unique, questions specific to your circumstances should be addressed to an appropriate professional to ensure that your situation has been evaluated carefully and appropriately. The author and the publisher specifically disclaim any liability or loss incurred as a consequence, directly or indirectly, of using and applying any of the concepts in this book.

ISBN: 978-0-9886710-2-7

TABLE OF CONTENTS

ACKNOWLEDGEMENTS

This book is dedicated to my parents, Bill and Donna, as well as my brother Billy, and grandfather Bill, for all of your unconditional love and support throughout my journey to become who I am today. This book is also dedicated in loving memory to my grandparents Marie Young, and Emily and William Martini.

Thanks to all my amazing clients that have inspired me to write about my passion.

Last, but not least; thank you to my very best accessory of all, my husband Hillel for all of your love and encouragement.

ABOUT THE AUTHOR

Ashley Martini, MBA, Styling Consultant, founding member of Martini Fashions, LLC, discretely assists both men and women unearth and exhibit their inner most beauty through style, fashion, and the top most trends. She graduated from Lynn University in Boca Raton, FL with a Business degree where she specialized in both fashion marketing and merchandising. She also completed her Masters in Business with a focus in International Business. She studied abroad in the world's fashion capital, Paris, France with a concentration in fashion styling and trend forecasting.

Ashley Martini vocationed as a styling intern with Jennifer Lopez's fashion company Sweetface/JustSweet/JLO. She has directed several Fashion Shows and has won numerous awards including the "Project Runway Competition" at Lynn University and the "Sak's Service and Selling Star Award" while employed as the Reed Krakoff Brand Ambassador at Saks Fifth Avenue. Her clothing has been featured in a variety of fashion shows. Additionally, she was hand picked to participate on the "NYC Prep" Television series in the episode titled, "The Overachievers." This episode featured upcoming stylists motivated and dedicated to succeed in the fashion industry.

Ashley Martini was born with a natural talent and an eye for style and impeccable taste. She has consulted several high-end business moguls, entrepreneurs, athletes, and celebrities.

Ashley Martini is currently working on futuristic fashion products that will be coming soon and available for purchase.

Ashley Martini is a native of Millbrook, NY, but now resides in Gulfstream, FL. She travels nationwide to ensure everyone looks his or her absolute best.

COMMIT TO LOOKING
YOUR BEST TODAY!

The benefit to working with a personal stylist is to maximize the impact of your wardrobe and add to your confidence level.

Call or E-Mail me Today! 1(914) 204-4198 | AM@AshleyMartini.com

or visit: www.AshleyMartini.com

The following are just some of the services that I can provide for you.

- **Fit Session** – A fit session involves a personalized assessment of both your body type and what will be most flattering on you.

- **Closet Consultation and Makeover** – I provide closet consultations, and makeovers utilizing my exclusive ASSERT closet organization process, while taking into account the comfort level of the client.

- **Personal Makeover** – In partnering with various salons and beauty/health service providers, I am able to facilitate clients who are seeking to find or refine a complete look.

- **Personal Shopping** – I will either provide a one-on-one shopping session or shop on my clients' behalf with specific client needs and requests in mind.

- **Bridal Styling** – This includes engagement photo styling, wedding dress shopping, groom's attire selection, bridal boudoir image styling, bridal party dress selection, and honey moon shopping

- **Event Styling** – By combining my personal shopping and makeover services it is possible for me to help transform you for the special events in your life

- **Men's Styling** – I provide all of my services for men, as well as ladies.

- **Maternity Styling** – Being pregnant does not mean having to give up style for 9 months. I am available for personal shopping and fit sessions for each trimester of your pregnancy to help ensure that you can be chic and confident during this time.

- **Children's Styling (newborn – 12 years old)** – I understand the needs of parents who want their children to be well dressed. I am available for closet consultations and modified personal shopping sessions for your children.

- **Teenage Styling (13 years old – 18 years old)** – I am available for both closet consultations and modified personal shopping sessions for your teenagers.

- **Editorial** – I am available for both commercial and fashion styling.

Introduction

"What you wear is how you present yourself to the world, especially today when human contacts are so quick. Fashion is instant language." - Muccia Prada

I tend to see people in terms of their outfits. Elements like a well-tailored suit or a perfect pencil skirt and accents like metallic pumps or studded bangles, all speak to me equally. This isn't a matter of passing judgment; it's inquiry, it's amazement, it's delight. It's how I respond to fashion and more importantly it's why I'm so drawn to style.

I can't always remember the last place I had a great lunch, tell you my first phone number or rattle off the names of Oscar winners. But I can recall in vivid detail the first pair of shoes that took my breath away, the emotion I feel when I put on my favorite dress and the desire to touch something that I can see is well made from a mile away.

Clothing and accessories offer each of us a unique magic, a chance to slip on armor or an invisibility cloak. They provide us the opportunity to cover ourselves in a portable love spell or to project a confidence that we may not feel but need to. These pieces are our masks and our mirrors. They're rites of passage and portals and offer us endless possibilities. You may not fully believe that now but you will by the end of this book.

Fashion and style are more than just my passions. They're a way of life. And for me, they always have been as if they are a part of my DNA.

My grandmother started buying clothes for me before I was born and currently her collection of costume jewelry, lush furs and fabulously unique pieces is mine.

I am the product of parents who greatly appreciated style. My father has always had impeccable taste and an appreciation for well made items. During their first Christmas as newlyweds he bought my mother a Fendi suit and a Gucci handbag, a reflection of both their fondness for craftsmanship. My mother is cut from a similar cloth and has always been passionate about fashion. She went to college to study fashion and dressed mannequins in local boutiques. She was particular in the way she dressed me while I was growing up.

And that brings it back to me again. A fashion plate from the beginning, my mother is fond of telling stories about how even as a little girl I wanted to wear what I wanted, when I wanted. Even now, a perfect day would be spent playing dress-up inside of an endless closet, pouring over fashion magazines. Part of my mission is to make you feel that rush as well, the exhilaration of a well put together outfit and a confident smile that's entirely your own.

My personal journey has taken me far from the closets of my childhood and into the real world. My studies have taken me to Paris where I was able to hone my styling and trend forecasting skills and have led me into an internship with Jennifer Lopez's fashion company Sweetface/JustSweet/JLO. Further work behind the "seams" has afforded me the opportunity to have my own clothing designs featured in numerous fashion shows while taking on the role of fashion show director for others as well. While employed with Sak's Fifth Avenue I was honored to receive the "Sak's Service Star" award for having great success as the Reed Krakoff brand ambassador. I was also asked to be in the buying department and was recruited by several companies. I've consulted with business moguls, entrepreneurs, athletes and celebrities, and now I'm pleased to be given the chance to work with you.

Consider the words on these pages your personal invitation into a world that exists all around you, enticing you to look at yourself, your closet, the way you shop, and what you wear in new and interesting ways. Allow them to coax you into embracing trends and to encourage within you a confidence that you deserve to feel.

And I'll be your tour guide.

Chapter one will allow us to get to know each other. And it's likely you'll learn a bit about yourself as well. While everybody has their own beauty, not every body is exactly the same. Before picking out clothes or making another purchase it's important you understand your body type and how to tailor your best fit.

Chapter two will build upon what we learned in chapter one about body types and take it one step further. If you're plus size, petite or tall, this chapter is tailor made for you and your styling needs.

Chapter three will take a look at the pieces that you should have in your wardrobe. Mix them and match them as you see fit for your own style but make sure you have them because it'll make getting dressed more enjoyable.

Chapter four is your chance to invite me into my favorite room in any house: the closet. This is your chance to show off, take stock and truly start taking ownership of the style choices you've made so far.

Chapter five is for the shopaholics in us all. Let me show you some of my favorite places online and off.

Chapter six is all about accessories, bangles, berets and booties: oh my! A complete outfit is about so much more than what you're wearing, it's also about the pieces that you choose to wear it with.

Chapter seven addresses the cost of retail therapy and takes a look at the pieces worth saving on and the ones you should indulge yourself and splurge on.

Chapters eight and nine are time to play dress up. Taking into account things like what body type you are and where you're going: it shows off some amazing outfits that you can use as your go to ensembles.

Chapter ten lets you relax and consider things like hair and skincare and why you should start pampering yourself right now.

Chapter eleven is for the guys and the great women who dress them.

Finally, take some time to look over some resources that I've taken years to compile. Everything from small shops that have great buys to new apps that'll make getting dressed more fun.

I'm ready to get started and I know you are too!

Chapter 1: Body Types

"Fashion is architecture. It is a matter of proportions."- Coco Chanel

We've all had that moment when we're browsing online, flipping through our favorite magazine or window shopping when we see "it". "It" is whatever in the moment we consider clothing perfection. "It" can be anything from a couture gown covered in jewels to a pair of skinny jeans. "It" is what we want, what we *need* as soon as we see it. But, as I'm sure you know, there's a fate worse than not being able to own "it".

Anyone who has looked at a piece of clothing with lust in their eyes and space in their closet knows the ache of not being able to take "it" home. The ache is multiplied, though, when it's not a matter of logistics or finance but rather one related to fit.

Just as we've all wished for certain pieces of clothing to magically appear in our closets, it's likely that we've also all stood in fitting rooms or our bathrooms or bedrooms full of loathing because that garment that had so much hanger appeal and looked so enticing on the model or mannequin looks less than stellar on us. While sometimes this is an issue of body image, it's often an issue of body type.

While your body image determines how you think you look, your body type describes how your body is shaped and therefore what will likely look most flattering on you. As this is the case it's important to know exactly what body type you have and how you can accentuate what's especially alluring about your shape.

Your body type is determined by a number of factors. These include things like your height and weight. It's also important to note that because of this your body type can change if your weight fluctuates, but it may not. Keep in mind that there are some women who will retain the same body type no matter how much weight they gain or lose, and others who will notice a dramatic shift. This has a lot to do with things like what parts of your body have a tendency to store fat and is partially a matter of genetics. Because you may have more than one body type throughout the course of your life, which is likely if you become pregnant or have plastic surgery, it's important that you have an awareness of what each body type is.

In total there are six basic female body types. These body types are labeled as the triangle, the inverted triangle, the rectangle, the diamond, the apple and the hourglass.

Women who fit into the **triangle** body type are generally more narrow above the waist. Generally this means that they have more narrow shoulders and that their chest is less full than their hips. Typically they carry more weight in their hip, butt and thigh areas. This body type is also called the pear type.

To best flatter your figure you want to create a greater sense of balance between your top and your bottom half. Try to avoid large, flashy belts or peplums instead opting for cleaner, smoother lines near your hips. Play up your smaller top half with bright colors, bold prints and structured shoulders.

Women who can be considered as having an **inverted triangle** body type have bodies that are the reverse of the triangle type body. While their hip and thigh areas are slim they have broader/fuller shoulders and chests.

To show off your shape consider pieces like a-line dresses which create the illusion of a fuller bottom half and are always stylish. Also, try pieces such as patterned or colored pants to draw more attention to your lower half while choosing solid colors for your top half.

Women with the **rectangle** body type generally have little definition in their waist or hips because their bust and hip measurements either are or appear to be equal. They also tend to have slim arms and legs. This body type is also labeled as athletic.

To showcase this style best you have to decide whether you're looking to show off your shape as it is, or if you're looking to accentuate the curves you do have. If you're into your body as is then opt for boxy or boy cut styles that look stunning on this body type. If you're trying to play up your curves, consider cinching or belting your dresses and tops to add definition.

Women who are classified as **diamond** body types tend to have a high sitting full stomach with wide hips and full thighs. Typically, they also have waistlines that are not well defined.

In order to best flatter your figure find pieces that fit well. Pieces that are baggy are only going to make you look bigger. Don't shy away from colors, prints or higher hemlines.

Women with **apple** body types are very similar to those with diamond body types. The key difference between the two is the stomach area. Women with this body type may have full stomachs that sit lower on their frame. This body type is also identified as the oval body type.

As a means of best dressing this body type, keep color and proportion in mind. While black is slimming and chic it can also be boring if it's the only color in your wardrobe. Play up your assets with v-neck tops and create a slimming effect with skinny, straight leg pants in any color.

Women with **hourglass** body types generally have bodies where their upper and lower halves are equal. Their bust and hip measurements match or look as if they do and their waists are well-defined.

This shape is often considered ideal, and as, such there are very few styles that don't flatter this figure. Keep in mind, though, that your pieces should still be well-fitting.

There are some of you who after reading the descriptions may be able to pinpoint exactly what your correct body type is and others who may feel as if they're not quite sure. No matter which category you fall into, I'm sure that you want to be 100% certain about your body type so that you can get the best possible advice for what's going to look most stellar on you.

In order to accurately assess your body type, you're going to need to honestly look at yourself in the mirror and focus on your hips, shoulders and waist. I suggest doing this in a bra and a pair of panties (no shapewear allowed) to ensure that you're looking at your body as it is, as opposed to how it looks in an outfit. To alleviate any distortions, make sure that the mirror is full-length and secure against a flat surface since a tilted mirror can skew what you see. If in doing this you're still not certain what shape you are, you may want to ask a friend you trust to help evaluate you.

While the above method is a good initial assessment, it's also important that you have your measurements taken. It's possible to do this yourself but for more accurate results you will want someone else to do this. This doesn't need to be done by a professional and can be done by a family member or one of your friends. If you want it done by a professional my suggestion is to call a local tailor or bridal salon and ask them if they have someone in house who can measure you and what the cost will be for this service. Similar to the mirror method, focus is placed on your hips, shoulders and waist. Additional emphasis is also placed on your bust area for a more complete idea of your body type. For each of these measurements you'll need flexible/fabric measuring tape. This can be picked up from most craft stores.

To measure your hips: In order to measure your hips you'll want to wear underwear (not shapewear) or form fitting pants or shorts such as leggings. You'll want to wrap the tape around the fullest part of your hips and butt for the most accurate measurement. Be sure to stand tall with your back straight and your heels together with your bare feet firmly on the floor. Make sure that the tape is neither too tight or too loose and bring together the two ends. The number in the center front is your hip measurement.

To measure your shoulders: To measure your shoulders keep your back straight and your shoulders relaxed. The tape should extend from the outer edge of one shoulder to the outer edge of the other. The number that appears on the second shoulder is your shoulder measurement.

To measure your waist: In order to achieve the most accurate waist measurement you'll want to wear your underwear (again no shapewear allowed). If you'd like to wear pants or shorts make sure that they are form fitting. To figure out where exactly to measure you'll want to bend forward and note where your body creases. This is your natural waistline and the area that you'll want to measure. Once you've located it return to standing up straight. It's important that you don't slouch and resist the urge to hold your breath or suck in your stomach. Bring the ends of the tape measure together in the center front of your body making sure that it's wrapped comfortably and not too loosely or tightly. The number in the center front is your waist measurement.

To measure your bust: Ensure that your'e standing up straight and wearing a form-fitting top or are topless. My suggestion is that you opt to wear a top that doesn't require wearing a bra underneath it, as many bras will alter this measurement. The tape needs to be wrapped across your back and under your shoulder blades and arms so that it's across the fullest part of your breast. This fit should be comfortable and not tight. Bring the ends of the measuring tape together in the center front and look at the number that falls there. This is your bust measurement.

After your personal assessment, the assessment of a friend and/or being measured, refer back to the descriptions and see where you fit. Remember that no matter what body type you keep, that there are clothes that will best flatter your figure, and the first step to figuring out what those clothes are is to find your body type.

Chapter 2: Plus size, Petite and Tall Tips

"There is nothing more rare, nor more beautiful, than a woman being unapologetically herself; comfortable in her perfect imperfection. To me, that is the true essence of beauty."- Steve Maraboli

I'm sure that you've heard the statement "Real women have curves". I kind of hate that statement. While it's true that real women do have curves it's also important to keep in mind that some women have smaller busts, some are tall with slender legs that look like they go on forever and some are built like ancient fertility goddess statues. And all of them are real women. Whether you're 4'11 or 5'9, 110 pounds, or 215 pounds you deserve to look and feel amazing. Shopping isn't always easy when you're plus size, petite or tall, but trust me when I tell you that there are some amazing clothes out there and by following the information in chapter 1 to determine your body type and coupling it with the do's and don'ts in this chapter, you're on your way to an amazing wardrobe.

Plus-size

Plus-size starts at a size 14. Keep in mind that sizes aren't standardized across brands, and so you likely have items in your closet that span a couple of sizes based on where or when they were purchased. Wearing a larger size doesn't mean you need to opt for minimal style.

Do highlight your assets. Things like shapely legs and well-toned arms are meant to be shown off so if you've got them, flaunt them.

Don't select fabrics that are bulky or overworked. Note that even sheer fabrics like chiffon can take on this quality if they're layered and/or ruffled.

Do seek out pieces that fit and flatter. Well-tailored clothing always looks amazing.

Don't shy away from bold colors or patterns. Large geometric prints, pretty floral patterns and bright colors can all be incorporated into your wardrobe. The key word here is bold. Keep in mind that with patterns, bigger is better when you're plus-sized.

Do be open to experimenting with different colors and trends. Working with a stylist can help you slowly ease pieces into your wardrobe that you may not pick out for yourself.

Don't forget to try pieces on. The fitting room is your friend and a trip there can be the difference between finding a piece that's amazing and taking home something that you'll ultimately have to return.

Do embrace plus size designers and plus size stores. No matter where you live you can almost always utilize an amazing online option if brick and mortar stores aren't an option.

Don't be afraid of layering. With items like tissue weight t-shirts and thinner sweaters, it's possible to layer your look and still look amazing.

Do make sure that your wardrobe is well-rounded. Select pieces that are appropriate for each season and for where you live and what your needs are.

Don't feel like you can't wear a swimsuit, a short skirt, a tailored jacket or a low cut top. All of those pieces exist as options.

Petite

Petite sizing isn't about weight, it's about height. There's some debate as to what the height range is, but it's been my experience that women 5'4 or shorter generally get the most benefit from petite styling advice.

Do realize that it's possible to be both petite and plus-size. This is especially important since clothes marked petite don't always reflect this.

Don't rely solely on clothing marked petite. Keep in mind that this is important whether you're plus sized or not. Some clothing that says it's for petite women will still be too long or in some cases it'll be too short.

Do opt for pieces that come in naturally shorter lengths. Cigarette pants, knee length or higher skirts and three quarter and shorter sleeve tops and jackets all show more skin and serve to make your limbs look longer.

Don't resort to quick fixes for your clothes. A simple cuff on the bottom of jeans or pants can look chic, but if you find yourself having to double and triple the cuff it's likely far too bulky. It's better to take your clothes to be altered by a professional.

Do dress age appropriately. A shorter stature makes some women feel as if they have to look matronly in order to be taken seriously, this is simply not the case.

Don't shop in the kids section to try and find pieces that will fit in terms of length. The clothes will not be cut appropriately and will make you look younger in a bad way.

Do embrace your height. This means it's okay to wear flats or sandals if that's what you're most comfortable in. There's no need for you to wear heels everywhere just to give you the illusion of height.

Don't avoid cut-outs or floor length pieces. It's possible for these items to look amazing on you and a stylist can help ensure that.

Do make sure that the proportions of the different pieces in your outfits are complimentary e.g. if you're wearing shorts don't wear a shirt that comes down too far past your waist.

Don't select clothing that's oversized, even if it happens to be on trend at the moment. Such pieces will always look too long even if their length is perfect on you and you'll look awkward.

Tall

Tall sizing is meant to cater to women who are 5'9 and taller and while this is the sizing of the average fashion model it can still be difficult for the average woman in this height range to find pieces that fit.

Do carefully read the care labels on all your clothes. This is especially important for tall women to ensure that the length you loved about a piece when you purchased it isn't ruined in the wash.

Don't discount how gorgeous you can look in Bermuda shorts, capris or cigarette length pants. While these are all tricky lengths to pull off they're not impossible.

Do wear high heels if you want to. Just because you're taller doesn't mean that this style of shoes is off limits.

Don't size up your clothes just to get a length that fits. While the length will be correct the overall look will ultimately be unflattering.

Do look at mens shoes if you're having difficulty finding something you love in your size. Consider that there are classic shoe shapes, like loafers and oxfords, that come in a surprisingly wide array of colors that would look stellar paired with jeans or tailored pants and a feminine shirt.

Don't assume that just because something is marked as being tall that it will fit you. Try the piece on or be prepared for the possibility of returning it.

Do opt for accessories that mirror your height. Longer earrings and necklaces help to create a look that's perfectly proportioned.

Don't slouch. Show off your height. This is good for your clothes as it helps to minimize wrinkles as well as your self-esteem, since you'll be walking with your head held high.

Do look for clothes that are made with a bit of spandex in them, the added stretch will help them fit your longer frame better.

Don't shy away from colors and patterns. Whether they're big and bold or muted and small, they'll likely look awesome on you.

Whether you're plus-size, petite, tall, or average you have to remember that there are amazing clothes available in your size that will also fit your body type. Working with a stylist can help you find these clothes so that you feel your most fabulous.

Chapter 3: Basics and Statements

"Create your style...let it be unique to you yet identifiable to others."- *Anna Wintours*

Fashion week is one of my favorite times of year. Getting to see what all the designers have on tap for the coming season makes me giddy. But the problem with trends is that they can be tricky. Sometimes it's a matter of personal taste, what you like as a consumer versus what designers are telling you is in. Sometimes it's a matter of being overwhelmed with selection and sometimes it's a desire to stick to what's comfortable and familiar. There's nothing wrong with any of that rationale. In fact, I'm encouraging you to embrace it. There's a time and a place to add some pizzazz to your wardrobe with a lush coat in the "it" hue of the moment, or to rush out and buy something covered in the current print or trim. And that time is after you've established a capsule wardrobe.

A capsule wardrobe is a wardrobe made up of fifteen-twenty pieces that can be mixed and matched. The beauty of building your own closet this way is that you always have something to wear. And while these certainly shouldn't be the only pieces you own, these should be the pieces that you always have on hand. The best capsule wardrobe is one that's a mix of basic and statement pieces, with some pieces that can be worn year round and others that are seasonal. If you make sure that you have these clothes and accessories on hand at all times you'll never find yourself unprepared, and will be perfectly dressed whether you're going out with the girls for drinks or only given a few minutes to pack for a surprise weekend getaway.

First things first. The basis of any good wardrobe is a good set of foundation garments. These pieces don't count toward the final twenty pieces of your capsule wardrobe but they should be the first ones that you buy. I believe in embracing your body and all it's curves but I also believe that when you look your best it's much easier to be your best. With that in mind, you have to make sure that what you're putting under your clothes helps to accentuate them as opposed to being a distraction. This is why if you choose to buy no other foundation garments you need to invest in a great bra, seamless underwear and a pair of Spanx.

Fact: a great bra does more than make your cleavage look amazing, it also serves to support your bust. There are a lot of women who have no idea what their real bra size is, and that's why I strongly suggest visiting a bra fit specialist before spending another dime on a bra that may or may not be the right size for you. I realize that may not be immediately possible so there are some things that you absolutely must keep in mind the next time you're out bra shopping. First, the bra should be secure but not tight, meaning that it should fit comfortably on the middle latch and that the straps shouldn't dig into your skin or feel loose. The underwire is meant to lay flat against your rib cage and the cups should be filled but not overflowing.

While you may like buying your bras and panties in sets, you'll also need to invest in separate seamless underwear. Also called no-show panties, these are a must-have if you like clothing that hugs your curves. There's no rule regarding color or cut, but you may need to try a few brands to find the most comfortable fit.

Spanx probably requires no introduction. The brand now makes everything from hoodies to skorts but when I talk about it, I'm talking about the original shapewear that the company started with. These body shapers can help create slimmer, sleeker lines and more importantly you can purchase one that's best suited for your body type since they have silhouettes that can trim the look of your thighs or stomach or enhance your butt. Plus, they come in three levels of slimming, ranging from medium to super-duper based on exactly how cinched you want to be.

The 10: Basic pieces that can be worn all year

There are 10 essential pieces that every wardrobe absolutely has to have. Will you have other clothes? Of course. But ensuring that you have these pieces means never having to worry about what you're going to wear.

1. Blazer: Blazers are everywhere from boardrooms to bars and while they may conjure up thoughts of prep schools what they really are, are secret weapons in any well-rounded wardrobe. You can cuff the sleeves and toss it over a fitted tee paired with jeans for a more pulled together casual look, pair it with a skirt for a customized suit or wear it over a dress for something more corporate, or over a corset paired with leather pants for a club look that's both edgy and interesting.

What to buy in your **20s**: Seek out quantity so that you have a few of these in your wardrobe. If you find and fall in love with something that's trendy then go for it, but make sure you also have one or two in more classic colors and styles as well. Also avoid anything with a school crest on it to avoid looking too juvenile.

What to buy in your **30s**: Opt for something that'll transition from an afternoon lunch meeting for work to meeting a date for drinks. This isn't about limiting your options but rather making sure you're not carrying around a carry-on with extra clothes. Spend some time finding a piece that fits well and is flattering.

What to buy in your **40s**: If you haven't already invested in a go to blazer that you love, now is the time. Chanel for example makes amazing iconic blazers and if you can't find a piece in the current collection that you love, look in reputable consignment shops for a gently worn secondhand piece that's perfect for you.

What to buy in your **50s**: Don't shy away from bright colors or bold patterns if you've spent years wearing more classic colors. However, keep in mind that you still want something that's going to wear well, which means that above all else the fit needs to be flattering.

If you're a **triangle** body type: Pick out a blazer that's either boyfriend-cut, which will look a little boxier and therefore create a more proportioned look, or look for something with slight shoulder pads.

If you're an **inverted triangle** body type: Try a blazer that has a little less structure. Softer fabrics will contour to your shape but won't add extra bulk.

If you're a **rectangle** body type: Look for a blazer that's belted or one that flares out slightly at the hips. These styles will help to better define your waist.

If you're a **diamond** body type: Opt for a blazer that looks better opened than it does buttoned. By leaving the blazer open you're less likely to draw attention to your mid-section.

If you're an **apple** body type: Try to find a blazer with slightly wider lapels that will frame your bust. Additionally, it may help to go a size up for a boxier look that will look polished whether you choose to wear it opened or buttoned.

If you're an **hourglass** body type: Search out a blazer that's fitted but not tight. Also look for blazers than have a bit of stretch in their fabric as that'll serve to better flatter your shape.

2. Cashmere duster or cardigan: I live in Cashmere dusters, especially when I travel. They look great, feel great and add a touch of luxury to every outfit. Wear one along with leggings and booties for a look that's casual and chic, or pair it with a sheath dress and pumps for a look that's both cozy and polished.

What to buy in your **20s**: While the color black is eternally fashionable and shades like cream and gray are always safe bets, don't be afraid to pick out something bolder.

What to buy in your **30s**: I personally love Calypso cashmere dusters. They come in a wide array of colors, and at around a $300, price point they're worth every penny. Buy one of these (or find a brand you love) and spoil yourself with something lush.

What to buy in your **40s**: My favorite duster comes from the Piacenza fabric mill in Biella, Italy. It was an investment piece that I was able to purchase while studying abroad. But more importantly, it's a piece that I truly love so I suggest you look for something that makes you feel the same way.

What to buy in your **50s**: Look for something functional that still makes you feel fabulous and can fit seamlessly into your routine.

If you're a **triangle** body type: Look for a duster that will lay over your hips and waist and help with the way your proportions look.

If you're an **inverted triangle** body type: Try a cardigan which when paired with plain pants or a skirt will serve to bring more of the focus to your upper body.

If you're a **rectangle** body type: Since dusters come in varying lengths, look for one that goes slightly past your waist but not as far down as your knees. The small amount of additional fabric near your waist and hips will help to create more flattering lines.

If you're a **diamond** body type: Opt for a cardigan or duster with a scoop neck or v-neck. Additionally look for one that belts as opposed to buttons for the most figure-flattering look.

If you're an **apple** body type: Look for a cardigan with a v-neck line and long sleeves. This silhouette will flatter your frame whether it's worn open or buttoned.

If you're an **hourglass** body type: Consider a cardigan or shorter duster if you're looking to show off your proportions. If you truly want a longer duster, opt for one that's belted.

3. Your favorite jeans: We all have a pair of jeans in our wardrobe that we love or a pair that we remember fondly because they were perfect and which we keep trying to replace with every new purchase. The jeans I'm talking about are the ones that you'll wear until you literally can't anymore. Denim is perfect paired with sneakers and a concert tee or dressed up with stilettos and a sequin tank, and 1,000 ways in between. Regardless of age or body type you want a pair that's quality so look for a pair that has a bit of spandex for stretch and buy them true to size.

What to buy in your **20s**: Now is the time to really experiment and find what works for you. Try different cuts and washes and look for the brands that fit you best.

What to buy in your **30s**: Keep in mind that darker washes and trouser jeans tend to be more work friendly. But if you don't find them flattering then don't bother.

What to buy in your **40s**: Avoid "mom jeans". This isn't meant to be a derogatory term, this is a catch all term that defines jeans that are high waisted in a way that isn't flattering on anyone. These may have a tapered leg, a pleat or an elastic waist and they genuinely don't look good on anyone.

What to buy in your **50s**: Once again avoid "mom jeans" and find a style that you love that looks good on your body.

If you're a **triangle** body type: A darker wash will work wonders at keeping you looking well proportioned. Additionally, avoid styles that have embellishments on the hips or back pockets.

If you're an **inverted triangle** body type: Consider denim in a lighter wash or one with wide belt loops that'll allow you to add a variety of belts that will draw attention to your waist. Straight leg jeans can be great but think twice about skinny jeans since, depending on what you pair them with, they may make your frame look more unbalanced.

If you're a **rectangle** body type: Check out a flattering high-waisted jean. This will work to rewrite the lines of your body. Or look into a boy-cut fit for a pair that best flatters your more athletic shape.

If you're a **diamond** body type: Stay away from jeans that are baggy or boxy or high waist as they'll likely look ill-fitting. Instead, seek out a straight legged, boot cut or skinny leg jeans.

If you're an **apple** body type: Look at jeans that range from boy cut to skinny and find a fit that flatters you. Low-rise jeans will generally be the least flattering.

If you're an **hourglass** body type: Check out straight leg or skinny jeans for the most figure flattering look. To minimize your curves try a more boxy cut.

4. An "Emergency dress": More commonly known as the little black dress, this is likely to be one of the most versatile pieces in your wardrobe.

Wear it with black pumps and a blazer to an interview or dress it up with bold stiletto heels and funky jewelry for New Year's Eve. Keep in mind that this dress is meant to be versatile, so avoid buying one with details that date it. Also, because it's likely to get a lot of wear, look for one with a fabric that breathes well and one that is well-fitting in the sense that it doesn't bunch when you sit and lays completely flat when you stand. Also opt for a more conservative length, looking for something that sits just above or just below the knee.

What to buy in your **20s**: This is the type of piece that you want to invest in so take the time to shop around and find a piece that will best fit in, in a variety of situations. Additionally, avoid anything that looks like it comes from a junior line such as puff sleeves, peter pan collars and shiny fabrics.

What to buy in your **30s**: This dress will likely be worn often so avoid anything that's too trendy in terms of shape or cut. Keep in mind that details aren't the only things which define and date a piece but so do hemlines and fabric choices. Additionally, choose something that will travel well.

What to buy in your **40s**: Look for something that's a bit more luxurious and bolder than what you typically wear. Just because this is a go-to piece that doesn't mean it shouldn't also be a head-turner. Try something in an always-in-style color like red or opt for something especially form fitting.

What to buy in your **50s**: Consider something in a slightly higher hemline with something not entirely expected and still elegant, and remember that it should fit your body well.

If you're a **triangle** body type: Consider cap sleeves and a square neckline which will help draw more attention to your upper body for greater balance.

If you're an **inverted triangle** body type: Look into an a-line dress which will add more fullness to your waist and hips.

If you're a **rectangle** body type: Opt for a sheath dress to show off your figure. To create more curves belt the dress with a wide belt in a deeper shade of black.

If you're a **diamond** body type: Try a dress with a slight a-line or one with a wide neckline as both will be most flattering to your figure.

If you're an **apple** body type: Consider a wrap style dress which is always fashionable. The v-neck line will look amazing and the belted, cinched or tied waist will best balance out your body.

If you're an **hourglass** body type: Look for a dress that has a more modest neckline and hem length. A fitted sheath would be incredibly flattering.

5. Black or nude pumps: Nude pumps are just as important as black ones in terms of their versatility in your wardrobe. While these shoes are of course in good company in a corporate setting they're also equally well received at cocktail hour. It may be tempting to pick out a sky high pump in faux pony skin, but opt for something more subtle in a man-made leather that will wear well repeatedly.

What to buy in your **20s**: It's okay to opt for something trendy provided it's also something functional. Also keep in mind all the places this shoe is meant to take you, then consider if you can honestly picture the one you're set on purchasing in each of those settings.

What to buy in your **30s**: Consider shoes that you can stand in, walk in and, if necessary, run for a cab in. Keep the heel height slightly lower and look for a shoe that's sturdy.

What to buy in your **40s**: Keep quality in mind as well as considering your comfort. You don't want a pair of shoes that you have to have resoled or replaced every few months or a pair that looks too tight on your foot.

What to buy in your **50s**: Think about trends cautiously and consider your own lifestyle. Find a shoe that not only fits you but fits in with what you're doing.

6. A comfortable ballet flat: This is such a classic shoe and equally as important to your wardrobe as a pump. Ballet flats pair well with everything from cigarette pants and a blouse to blue jeans and a tank top.

What to buy in your **20s**: Look for something that's lightweight and find a neutral color or pattern.

What to buy in your **30s**: Consider something slightly dressier which makes them easier to pair with everything.

What to buy in your **40s**: Quality is key. You want flats that'll wear well in all weather.

What to buy in your **50s**: Don't feel restricted by color or pattern and pick out a few pairs that you love.

7. Sunglasses: Sunglasses offer the perfect cover when you don't feel like primping but still want to look pulled together while out running errands. Add a touch of lip gloss for a nearly effortless look that's still chic.

8. A crisp white t-shirt or white button-down: Both of these are classic pieces which pair well and wear well with almost everything else in your wardrobe. Look for pieces that are pre-shrunk and that feature natural fibers for the most flattering fit.

What to buy in your **20s**: A great white tee is something that you have to have. Paired with your blazer, blue jeans and ballet flats you have a look that's preppy without being pretentious. Paired with yoga pants and sneakers it's lounge wear that still looks good.

What to buy in your **30s**: If you feel the need to choose between the tee and the button-down pick the button down every time. Worn with a suit it's suitable for the office or paired with a ball gown skirt, similar to the signature personal style of designer Carolina Herrera, is perfect for a more upscale event.

What to buy in your **40s**: Get both the tee and the button down. Look for a tissue weight tee that can be layered more easily under form fitting cardigans, etc. and opt for a button-down that has a bit of stretch.

What to buy in your **50s**: Consider some different fabrics. While cotton and cotton blends are generally the most comfortable pieces also look for pieces made from silks and sheers for a look that's a bit more interesting.

If you're a **triangle** body type: Look for a tee or a button-down with a more interesting neckline to draw the eye to the top half of your body.

If you're an **inverted triangle** body type: Consider a tee or a button-down that sits at or slightly below your hips as it'll serve to make you look your most flattering.

If you're a **rectangle** body type: Get a tee or a button-up that is form fitting and specifically cut for women. You don't want pieces that are too boxy.

If you're a **diamond** body type: Opt for a tee or button-up that fits well but isn't tight. Pieces that have some stretch may be ideal.

If you're an **apple** body type: Look for tees that have a v-neck and button up shirts that have some stretch. Make sure that the piece you purchase fits well.

If you're an **hourglass** body type: Look for a tee or button up that's slightly boxy and try a scoop neck or demure v-neck.

9. A classic handbag: When I refer to a classic handbag I'm not necessarily referring to iconic pieces like the Chanel quilted bag or the Hermes Birkin. Instead, I'm referencing a bag that makes the most sense for your daily life, whatever that may entail.

What to buy in your **20s**: Sometimes all you need is a cute clutch and other times a tote works best. For this bag in particular look for something that's in between those two things. It may be tempting to go with an "it" color or a bag similar to the one your favorite celebrity carries and I'm not saying not to get that bag. You just need to seriously assess if it's going to work for you.

What to buy in your **30s**: Whether you're a working woman, super mom or somewhere in between, you want a bag that will work effortlessly with almost any outfit. Select a more neutral shade like black or navy that will coordinate with the pieces you have rather than clashing with it.

What to buy in your **40s**: Consider something that can go from day to evening. Also, look for interesting accents that aren't overwhelming. Great hardware and interesting straps all lend a bit of interest without being overpowering.

What to buy in your **50s**: Pick something that suits your lifestyle and speaks to your taste. Don't get hung up on aspects like color and consider if it has enough compartments and if it complements your style.

10. Your perfect accessory: Maybe you love being draped in pearls. Perhaps you adore a bold cocktail ring. This piece needs to be all about you, something in which the instant you put it on you feel flirtatious and fearless. For me, my personal go-to is a pair of diamond studs which are both glamorous and understated, and go as well with a pair of jeans as they do with an evening gown. No matter what age you are, keep searching until you find something signature.

Seasonal additions

As the seasons come and go, you need to consider refreshing your wardrobe. This means adding in some additional basics based on what the weather is likely to be like outside. Some of these pieces may come and go as trendy, but their true value lies in the fact that after other trends have faded they'll still be fashionable.

Summer: Summer is often a season spent outdoors and on the go. You want clothes that are light and effortless, and that still look polished.

1. A little white dress: Consider this your second emergency dress and shop accordingly. Keep in mind that while linen is a great fabric because it breathes beautifully, that it also wrinkles easily. It may only be a good choice if you know that you'll never need to just throw this piece in your bag and go.

2. A wide-brimmed hat: This piece is perfect because it does double duty. Not only does it shade your eyes but it also adds a bit of mystery. As a bonus the simple addition of a light-weight scarf tied just above the brim can dress this piece up.

3. Sunscreen: While sunscreen isn't an accessory in the conventional sense, it's still essential no matter how old you are or what your skin tone or type is.

In your **20s**: Add sandals and denim cut-offs. I know that flip flops can be comfortable but they're not always appropriate. Instead, opt for a pair of espadrilles which are just as comfortable and far more chic. In terms of the denim cut-offs, follow similar guidelines to the ones for finding your perfect pair of jeans and look at different washes.

In your **30s**: Add a woven beach tote and a versatile cocktail dress. The right beach tote can take the place of your classic handbag while you're out soaking up the sun. A good cocktail dress can take you from brunch with old friends to dinner at a four-star restaurant. Follow the same guidelines as those given for the emergency dress except look for something at cocktail length and in a color that flatters you.

In your **40s**: Add caftans and jeweled sandals. Both of these pieces add an air of instant elegance with no fuss. Plus, they both transition well from day to night.

In your **50s**: Add a well-fitting bathing suit and lightweight pants. Finding a bathing suit that fits well can be akin to finding the perfect foundation garments. Regardless of body type you want something that flatters your figure and so it's worth shopping around until you find the perfect piece. While pants of any kind may initially seem out of place in this season, something ultra lightweight will work well on cooler summer evenings when you may be out or entertaining.

Fall: Fall is crisp and a bit cold, and while you want to be cozy you may still be craving the ability to wear pieces more suited for warmer weather or looking forward to the ability to layer pieces. Either way, what's required are some additions to your wardrobe that allow you to mix and match.

1. A boyfriend sweater: A boyfriend sweater is by nature a piece that's boxier than what you'd normally wear and it can look flattering on every body type. If you have broader shoulders and/or a fuller bust or mid-section, opt for a cardigan to help better distribute the extra volume. If you're looking to draw more attention to the top of your frame then try a more traditional sweater with a v-neck. While you can certainly pick this piece up in the men's department, many stores also sell this style in the women's department.

2. A suede skirt: There's something timeless about a suede skirt. Ankle length and worn with high heeled boots it's chic, and short worn with a pair of flats it's cute. Hemline is, however, not as important as color and for this season you'll want to select something darker.

3. Booties: Ankle boots or booties are as adorable as they are versatile. Look for a pair in a suede or man-made leather and opt for a neutral tone such as black or chocolate brown to ensure you'll be able to wear them frequently.

In your **20s**: Add a fur vest and corduroy shorts. Whether it's real or faux, a fur vest is a great addition to your fall wardrobe. It'll pair well with your jeans and add a bit of polish over a plain tee. Corduroy shorts, while not immediately expected, look awesome over patterned or textured tights with a light sweater.

In your **30s**: Add riding boots and a trench coat. Both of these pieces are iconic in their own right and denote a sense of luxury and status. Look for pieces that not only fit well but that are made well.

In your **40s**: Add a little navy dress and a pair of red pumps. The little navy dress is crisp and chic. Shop for it like you'd shop for your emergency dress. Red pumps add a bit of instant color to a black or gray suit and allow you to stand out without showing off.

In your **50s**: Add a pencil skirt and a cape coat. Pencil skirts are their sleekest at about mid-knee and a woman in such a skirt immediately looks powerful and posh. This is a style that's wearable by every body type. If you're looking to define your waist opt for one with a wider band or one that can be belted. If you're looking to minimize the look of your mid-section look for something with a bit of stretch. Cape coats are also flattering on every body type as well as being able to add a bit of elegance to every look.

Winter: The fact that it's cold outside is no excuse for your clothes to be boring. Pieces for this season should certainly be warm but stylish as well.

1. Little black sweater dress: When purchasing this piece keep the words of Tim Gunn in mind, noting that if you have to ask whether something is a top or a dress that it's always a top.

2. Tights: Tights don't have to be purely functional. Look at pairs that come in vibrant colors or ones with interesting textures.

3. Leather gloves: Aside from being sleek and a bit sexy, leather gloves also make for an incredibly practical purchase. Make sure that they're lined for extra warmth.

In your **20s**: Add fur neck scarves and warm boots. Both of these pieces are meant to be functional and can also be highly fashionable. Choose real or faux fur, depending on your preference, and look for a boot that is comfortable.

In your **30s**: Add a tweed blazer and a knee-length leather skirt. Both tweed blazers and leather skirts, add a bit of texture to your wardrobe. Even if you opt for them in neutral tones they'll still both standout. Follow the blazer guidelines for your body type noting that a fabric like tweed can add extra bulk. When looking for a leather skirt, avoid any temptation that may exist to go for a higher hemline as you're looking for a piece that'll work both in the office and on a date. My suggestion is to stick with a black or chocolate brown, but if you absolutely must have color go for a gray which is still very classic.

In your **40s**: Add a tailored pea coat and a wool sweater. The key with both of these pieces is fit. Don't settle for anything that isn't 100% flattering.

In your **50s**: Add a low-heeled closed-toe slingback shoe and a fur muff. Heels can be worn year round but a lower heel height tends to be better for the winter. Feel free to consider different colors and fabrics. For the fur muff, whether it's real or faux, it'll look fabulous and add a bit of immediate glamour with little effort.

Spring: Spring is a great season for clothes that are bold and bright. Since it's a transitional season you want to avoid clothes that look like they are too warm or beach ready.

1. A printed wrap dress: A printed wrap dress offers a great mix of color and pattern in one easy to wear package. Diane Von Furstenberg makes pieces that you can wear until the end of time that will always be fashionable and as such are worth the investment. As a bonus, wrap dresses look amazing on every body type.

2. Earrings you adore: Whether you're into studs or hoops, spring offers the perfect time to show off your earrings. You may find a signature pair that you pair with everything or you may choose to rotate a few pairs based on mood and outfit.

3. Light colored jeans: Light colored jeans are an awesome addition to any wardrobe for Spring. Whether you select a lighter wash of blue or something more bold in terms of a pretty pastel or primary color, you want to follow the same guidelines for picking out your perfect pair of jeans.

In your **20s**: Add a maxi dress and a jean jacket. Maxi dresses and jean jackets are pieces that are both timeless and youthful. When selecting the dress don't feel limited by color or patterns. Follow the basic fit guidelines for the emergency dress, disregarding the notes relative to length and simplicity. When picking out a jean jacket don't try to match the denim to your favorite jeans, instead select a medium wash that will look great in place of your blazer for events that are ultra casual.

In your **30s**: Add white jeans and deck shoes. White jeans and deck shoes look grown-up and sophisticated without coming across as old. In terms of fitting the jeans, follow the guidelines for finding your perfect pair. For the deck shoes, look for something that's comfortable and also fits your signature style. If you're more introverted you may want a pair in neutral or navy and if you're extroverted you may be interested in a bolder color or print.

In your **40s**: Add dark tailored trouser jeans and a silk shell top. While light colored jeans are amazing for the spring time they aren't always appropriate e.g. they may be out of place in the office and so your pair of dark tailored trouser jeans can stand in, in those instances. Additionally, a silk shell top is much more chic than a tank and will take you effortlessly from a morning meeting to a night on the town.

In your **50s**: Add a shawl or a wrap and kitten heels. Spring weather is still slightly unpredictable so having a shawl or wrap on hand ensures that you can always get rid of the chill. Kitten heels are sweet and practical as they can be paired equally well with a great skirt or a capri pant.

Statement pieces

Statement pieces transcend age and body type. These are the little extras that every woman should have on hand for an extra bit of elegance and edge.

1. Oversized clutch: A clutch is the quintessential bag for a night out yet not always the most practical for a woman who totes around more than her keys, lipstick and phone. The solution is an oversized clutch, something that's still undeniably an evening bag with just a bit more room. Remember that this is meant to be a statement piece so don't be shy about finding something that's studded, covered in Swarovski or in an amazing animal print or interesting color.

2. A great leather jacket: A leather jacket that you love is a piece you'll never regret buying and it's a piece where your body type isn't truly an issue. Just look for something that fits well that you feel amazing in.

3. Black Louboutin pumps: The pumps are more about fashion than function, although they do wear incredibly well. With a proprietary blood red sole they're instantly recognizable.

4. Chanel pearls or a cocktail ring: Both pearls and cocktail rings convey a bit of instant luxury. Also, there are a myriad of affordable options, especially in terms of the latter. Look for a piece that you genuinely love.

5. Red lipstick: There's not a woman in the world who doesn't instantly feel a bit more like a femme fatale with red lipstick on, and moreover there's a shade that looks good on every skin tone.

Your secret weapons

No matter what you're wearing it'll look a million times better if you pair them with both of these pieces.

1. A killer smile: It may seem a bit saccharine but the next time you're having a bad day just stop and try to smile. It's silly but it really does help to brighten your face and lighten the mood.

2. An amazing attitude: There are going to be genuinely bad days, experiences that are crushing and moments when you want to give up. The ultimate goal, though, should be to get past those moments and, moreover, to be as fabulous as possible while doing it.

Style isn't just about the clothes you wear or the things you buy, it's also about how you feel. A stylist can help to unlock not just the best looking you, but the best you, period.

Chapter 4: Closet Organization

"Big: Should we get you a diamond?

Carrie: No, please don't get me a diamond...get me a really big closet." - Sex and the City

We've all had that moment when we looked into our closets, and despite the amount of clothes inside, felt like we had nothing to wear. It seems contradictory but it's a completely valid argument since sometimes what we have in our closets aren't exactly the right pieces for our wardrobes.

When I talk about the right pieces, I don't mean what's on trend for the season or pieces that for whatever reason you're supposed to love. Instead, the right pieces are the ones that fit and flatter, and are complimentary to your current lifestyle. Anything that doesn't meet that criteria, no matter how beautifully made, well-tailored or new is unfortunately wrong, at least for now.

Simply looking in your closet doesn't really provide you with any insight regarding which pieces are right, and therefore worth keeping and which pieces are wrong, and therefore should be let go of. In order to assess this you need to tackle a closet organization process. There are numerous ways in which this can be done but I've found that the best method is a simple 6 step process I've dubbed the A.S.S.E.R.T method which allows you to truly go through each piece of clothing.

Let's get started:

A: Assess

Assessing what's in your closet can be daunting, especially if you have a lot of items. But it'll help you be honest about who you are versus what your style is saying, which unfortunately isn't always harmonious.

Take a good look at each piece and consider the following three questions:

1) When did I buy this?

2) Why did I buy it?

3) How often do I wear it?

The answers to these questions can be very telling. Consider that if you bought something years ago on impulse and have never worn it that it's likely not worth the closet space it's taking up, especially when compared to a piece that you wear fairly frequently or that you bought recently and may not yet have had a chance to wear.

S: Sort

Having taken the time to honestly assess your clothes it's now possible to sort them into more manageable piles. This can be done based on season or if your wardrobe for the year isn't immediately accessible in your main closet, then sort the clothing based on activity, such as the clothes you wear to work, the clothes you wear on dates and the clothes that you wear for running errands.

S: Sort (again)

Working with your individual piles, take the time to go through them each again. What you're looking to weed out specifically is anything that doesn't fit, anything that needs mending and anything that is stained. Consider carefully if any of these items are worth saving. For example, a dress that you love that hangs more loosely than the fit intends can likely be taken in by a tailor whereas if you find a hole in a pair of pants that you're not really fond of you may wish to get rid of them.

E: Eliminate

Look through the clothing that you've weeded out and carefully consider what's wrong with it. If the issues are superficial e.g. you no longer personally love the color, the piece isn't on trend, or the piece simply doesn't fit with your current style then commit to taking the time to donate these pieces. Keep in mind the style of clothing and make donations accordingly. For example, if you're getting rid of clothing that can be worn in an office or on a job interview then look for a local women's shelter or halfway house that can immediately make the clothes available to its residents. Similarly, if you have evening gowns that you're getting rid of you should attempt to seek out a charity that provides prom dresses for under-privileged young women. While this may take some extra time it will ensure that the clothing goes where it can be of the most use. Of course, if the clothes are completely unwearable you'll likely want to trash them, but I suggest making a call to your recycling center and see if they have the option to recycle them first.

R: Reorganize

Making sure that the clothes you're donating or giving away are completely separate, it's time to put your clothes back in your closet. Take the time to put them back in with care, keeping them in the same groups which you've sorted them into. This will make pieces much easier to find in the future. Additionally, make sure that all of the hangers are facing in the same direction. When you wear a piece, put it back in the closet facing in the opposite direction. If you wear it more than once change the color hanger that it's on.

T: Take inventory

Let three months pass and look in your closet once again. Look specifically at anything that isn't a basic or statement piece, and consider how many times you've worn the item and how likely you are to wear it within the next month.

Following these 6 steps will provide the true measure of what your personal style is versus what you may proclaim it to be. In doing this you may realize that your style is a bit more elegant than you initially assumed or that you have pieces that you adore that don't exactly fit into your lifestyle. Or any one of a hundred other things. Keep in mind that there is no absolute right answer to this, nor is any answer wrong. With that it mind it's up to you to decide what you want to do with this knowledge and how you'd like to move forward. You may realize that you have a much clearer style vision than you originally gave yourself credit for. Keep in mind, that hiring a stylist can help you hone in on the exact style P.O.V. that you want to present to the world.

Chapter 5: Personal Shopping

"Buy what you don't have yet. or what you really want, which can be mixed with what you already own."-Karl Lagerfeld

Every piece you own has a story. Maybe there are a pair of shoes that you pre-ordered months in advance to ensure you would have them. Or perhaps there's a dress in your closet that you never planned on buying but that you had to have after glancing at it in a boutique window. We all have at least one piece that we bought simply because it made us smile and a few that were banished to the back of the closet shortly after getting them home because we're not sure what we were thinking when we handed over our credit cards or cash and let them into our lives in the first place. Our closets are not only filled with our clothes, they're also filled with our memories and sometimes our mistakes. Half of the battle in eliminating wardrobe missteps is knowing where to shop and what types of things to buy when you get there. To guide you, this chapter is separated to include insight on both brick-and-mortar establishments as well as online options.

Department Stores

Department stores are amazing places, expansive and inviting. They carry everything from cocktail dresses to cookware. For some people, they can be daunting but savvy shoppers are able to go in, get what they want and go home happy.

How to get the most from your experience: Whether you're in a luxury department store like Saks or someplace more accessible like Macy's, my suggestion is that you select something from a designer you're not wholly familiar with but whose aesthetic speaks to you. Because department store price points are slightly lower compared to what you may find elsewhere they offer a great opportunity to explore and expand your style.

What to avoid: Since style is such a personal thing stay away from any item that is available in a rainbow of colors unless it's an absolutely basic piece like a blazer. Additionally, no matter how great the price is stay away from anything that doesn't feel good or look good against your skin.

Flagship stores

If you live in or shop in cities like Boca Raton or Los Angeles you've likely been in a flagship store. These are stores featuring a single designer and as such are the perfect destination for anyone especially devoted to a particular label.

How to get the most from your experience: These locations are destinations and they know it. As such, be sure to take full advantage of any amenities that are offered as a result of visiting the brick-and-mortar location as opposed to shopping online. Keep in mind that such perks will vary by location. For example, if you go to the Armani flagship store on 5th avenue in New York, it's possible for you to dine in the Armani Ristorante, an eatery within the store itself. Other flagship stores offer other options such as exclusive salons, appointment only tailoring or opulent lounge areas.

What to avoid: Unless it's the whole purpose of the visit, try not to pick up anything too basic. With the exception of items like t-shirts that may be flagship store exclusives, it's likely that the more basic the piece the more readily available it will be elsewhere. Utilize this time to both enjoy the overall ambiance and check out pieces that you may not have seen before or may not have access to elsewhere.

Boutiques

Boutiques generally offer a mix of emerging and well-known designers in a smaller space. These locations showcase carefully curated pieces and may feature a mix of regional and local designers alongside those that you already know and love.

How to get the most from your experience: You're going to want to do some research beforehand. Because of their smaller sizes boutiques are not as well stocked as department or flagship stores. While you can certainly walk into one at random and find something you love, it's just as likely that you may find yourself completely turned off. This means that in advance you need to call or look up the shops online and see what designers they carry and what size range they have. Don't rely solely on their online presence to give you this information as it may not reflect their most recent buys. One easy way to avoid this extra bit of hassle is to hire a stylist to act as your personal shopper, then they'll be the one who does any necessary legwork in advance to help ensure that where you're shopping is suited to you.

What to avoid: Unless you're working with a trusted stylist who has made arrangements for you to try on specific types of pieces, it's best to go into a boutique shopping situation with an open mind about what may be available. There'll be times when you'll find an array of great pieces and instances where you may only find one item you like. Additionally, don't make presumptions about what you think their policies are or should be. Before you buy anything find out if and how they handle returns.

E-boutiques

E-boutiques are a lot like their brick-and-mortar counterparts in that they carry amazing designer pieces and tend to be easy to navigate. While many of these sites carry well-known designer labels, there are also some that cater to more indie brands, a mix which generally means that your own wardrobe will have more freshness and personality.

How to get the most from your experience: Try and limit your perusal on e-boutiques to no more than two or three per day. Keep in mind that online shopping is still shopping, and so it's still possible to get overwhelmed by what's being presented. A stylist can help you find specific sites that carry pieces that'll complement your body type and your personality.

What to avoid: Unless you're familiar with the way a particular brand will fit, don't follow the listed sizes. Sometimes the differences between designers is minimal and other times it's the difference between a piece that's immediately wearable and one that you'll have to wait to be altered.

International e-boutiques

As amazing as it would be to catch a flight to Paris every single fashion week or spend a Friday morning shopping in another country, it's simply not feasible. Thank goodness for the Internet and its vast offering of amazing shopping sites from other parts of the world.

How to get the most from your experience: Truly embrace the option of having access to designers that may not be available locally. When shopping this way, it's encouraged to look for pieces both from well-known designers whose lines may be limited stateside and for work by designers who aren't familiar to you but who have pieces that'll flatter you.

What to avoid: Be incredibly aware of the fact that sizes are cut differently overseas and will vary from country to country. This is especially important when looking at pieces from Asian retailers, which are sized much smaller than their European counterparts. Almost all international sites have detailed size charts available that you should check carefully before ordering.

Trunk shows

Trunk shows are special events where designers are presenting their wares specifically to consumers or store buyers. This differs from a department store or boutique setting in the sense that the selection is generally much more tightly curated and there is a possibility that you will be interacting with the designer themselves or a direct representative of the line. There is no specific place for these sales, per se, but keep in mind that Henri Bendel hosts them in New York frequently as a way to introduce newer designers to the public.

How to get the most from your experience: If you're not an experienced trunk sale shopper you're going to want to get the assistance of a stylist who has navigated these events beforehand. In working with that individual, the two of you can discuss the types of things that you're looking to purchase as well as your general availability to attend an event of this type. Keep in mind that there will likely be no fitting rooms or returns. A stylist can tell you exactly how to dress to ensure that this isn't an issue. Also, even more so than boutique shopping, there is a lot of legwork that needs to be done in order to ensure that even if you ultimately don't purchase anything that your shopping experience is a pleasant one.

What to avoid: Don't be indecisive. Consider that what you see at a trunk show likely isn't available elsewhere. This is especially true if the designer presenting the pieces is emerging as opposed to established. If you see something you adore, this is the time to buy it but only if it's good quality. Additionally, don't be afraid to ask questions. For example, if you see a dress that you have to have but the size is off ask the designer to quote you a price for the same piece fitting your measurements. If the pricing is agreeable, exchange information so that you can follow up after the event.

Designer sample sales

Designer sample sales come in two varieties. There are the sales that are open to the public and occur throughout the year and there are those that are private, by appointment only and can often be scheduled to suit your needs. Public sales tend to offer a mix of merchandise in a variety of sizes, and are generally held either in-store or in an offsite location to accommodate all of the people in attendance. Private sales generally have fewer pieces, however, these pieces are hand-selected by the designer, often with the help of a stylist to appeal to the purchaser. These pieces may only be available in sample sizes or unfinished and therefore it may not be possible to try them on, but if a purchase agreement is made the final garments will be tailored to fit. In both cases, a stylist is recommended and in the latter case a stylist will definitely be needed unless you personally know the designer and can make the arrangements on your own.

How to get the most from your experience: Public sample sales can be crazy. There are often no fitting rooms, long lines and the merchandise doesn't stay orderly. If shopping truly was a sport these sales would be Olympic style events. A stylist can help guide you to the sales that you're most likely to be pleased by and a personal shopper on hand can offer an extra set of eyes to ensure that nothing you're about to buy has been ripped, stained or otherwise damaged during the evening. This is crucial since there are no returns. In a private sale setting be sure that you discuss beforehand what you're looking for. This will allow the designer to put together the best rack possible.

What to avoid: Neither situation is going to be pleasant if you're timid. In a public setting, it's likely that you'll need to raise your voice if it's especially crowded. In a private setting, if you're not seeing pieces that you like, politely let the designer know as he or she may have other samples available to show you or may be able to offer alterations on what they're presenting. This is especially true if the issue is something relatively small such as wanting a slightly higher hemline.

Customized and Limited edition shopping

There's only one surefire way to ensure that you're the only one in the room with a certain piece on, and that's to make sure that you're the only one who has it at all. The Internet offers quite a few options for you to create and find pieces that are either completely unique to you or produced in very small quantities. While in many ways this is similar to designer sample sales, it has the added benefit of adding pieces to your wardrobe that are extra special.

How to get the most from your experience: Open yourself up to pieces from little-known designers or companies. Additionally, when you're having something custom made take the time to work with the designer to ensure that the final piece is something truly special.

What to avoid: When it comes to having a custom piece created or scouting for something limited edition, indecision is the enemy. If you only have a vague idea of a garment you want created you have two options. The first is to hold off until your vision becomes clearer. The second is to work with a stylist to help you identify shapes, silhouettes and colors that look amazing on you. If you're looking at limited edition items, realize that hesitation may mean that it ends up with someone else so if you really love it then you may need to buy it right when you see it.

Members only shopping sites

Sometimes you don't know exactly what it is you want until you see it and members only sites specialize in showing off their goods. By signing up for one of these kind of sites you're granted access to shopping in a different way. Many offer daily emails, flash sales and, in some cases, pieces that are exclusive to them.

How to get the most from your experience: Look for sites that will let you preview what they have available for signing up. While some sites will only let you see a list of the designers they carry, others will let you look at the actual items that they have available. Once you've decided which sites to join, keep in mind which ones only offer items for a limited amount of time. With sites like these you may need to be prepared to choose quickly whether or not you want an item. You may want to have a stylist scour these sites beforehand to avoid impulse buys you may not be in love with later on.

What to avoid: Don't forget to read the terms of the sale. Consider that for some sites you'll be pre-ordering pieces that will not ship immediately.

Consignment stores

Consignment stores can be incredible. I'm personally a huge fan of this type of shopping because it's possible to find some amazing pieces that aren't currently being produced and the quality is often stellar.

How to get the most from your experience: Ensure that where you're shopping is a reseller of luxury goods and that they don't sell knock-offs. Keep in mind that they don't need to sell high-end pieces exclusively, but whatever designer pieces they sell should be authentic. A good stylist will often know the best places in your area to go so getting their help will be a huge asset.

What to avoid: Stay clear of thrift stores. While they also resell goods, the dynamics of how it's done are different. Consignment stores only present the best items they have access to because their merchandise is purchased from consigners which allows them to be more selective. Thrift stores, on the other hand, have all of their merchandise donated and as such the same level of quality control isn't in place. It's possible to find something amazing in these places, but it's much more probable that even after an entire afternoon of shopping that you'll still be empty-handed.

Regardless of the shopping experience, choosing a great stylist or personal shopper can make it especially worth your while. Their talent and expertise will help you best navigate where to go so that you'll be your most comfortable and confident in whatever pieces you ultimately purchase.

Chapter 6: Shoes and Accessories

"Accessories are important and becoming more and more important every day. They can completely change the look of an outfit, and women like the idea of having a wardrobe that's versatile. For instance, a strong piece of jewelry can make a simple outfit look elegant." - *Giorgio Armani*

No outfit, no matter how fabulous or fashionable the clothes may be, can ever truly be considered complete without a pair of shoes and an accessory or two. This applies for every outfit whether you're pairing a bold bangle and stilettos with a red dress for an evening out or slinging a gym bag over your shoulder as you head out to meet with friends for a workout. Considering this, it's highly important to understand some basics about these pieces and how they can enhance rather than overwhelm an ensemble.

Shoes

There's nothing quite like the right pair of shoes. Whether it's a casual pair of flats or a fantastic pair of stilettos, shoes act as a way of making a brilliant outfit even better. While shoes show up in almost every venue that offers clothing, there's a broader selection available if you seek out stores and sites that are more specifically geared towards this staple.

How to get the most from your experience: Do a bit of research beforehand or work with a stylist who'll do the legwork for you in order to ensure that the stores or sites that you're visiting both have the styles of shoes you like and a great selection of sizes. Also, try to go shoe shopping in the middle of the day to ensure a truer fit as our feet swell throughout the day and are at their largest around this time.

What to avoid: Never buy a pair of shoes that's ill-fitting, either too big or too small just because you have your heart set on that particular style or brand.

While women's shoes can basically be separated into two categories: heels and flats, any true fashionista knows that the subcategories are much more varied than that, although sometimes it can be hard to navigate what type of shoe works for what occasion or what outfit type. While working with a stylist directly will help you to find the exact shoes that should be incorporated into your personal wardrobe, what follows is an overview of some of the more common shoe shapes, what they look best with and where they'll fit in.

Ballerina flats

Ballerina flats are incredibly versatile, they may be completely flat or have a small heel. These types of shoes can be perfectly paired with items like straight leg jeans, a lace edged camisole and a comfortable cardigan for a relaxed weekend look, or worn with a short full skirt and fitted v-neck t-shirt for a lunch date. No matter where you live or what your lifestyle is like, it's likely that you'll need a pair or two of these kind of shoes and considering that they come in an amazing array or colors, fabrics and patterns, you're bound to find something that suits your personality. One of my favorite brands Repetto, a company that originated in Paris, makes incredible ballet flats that wear very well.

Sandals

Sandals come in a variety of forms from the super casual flip flop which works well with cut-offs and an off the shoulder top for a day at the beach to dressier gladiator style sandals which can be paired with a plain or printed maxi dress for a modern day Grecian inspired look. Depending on where you live, these shoes may only be worn during the summer but that doesn't mean that you shouldn't own at least one pair. My suggestion is that you either select a pair that transitions from day to night or look for at least two distinct pairs, one that you can wear while running errands and another that's more of an evening shoe. Additionally, keep in mind that jeweled sandals offer an amazing dressed up option for women who can't or don't want to wear heels.

Boots

There are so many different types of boots. There are classics, like the flat riding boot, which look amazing worn with skinny jeans and a cable knit sweater in the fall and newer styles, like the Lita boot, with which its chunky heel and wide hue availability present a styling wild card which allow wearers to flaunt truly unique looks. Consider that even if you live in a warmer climate that a pair of boots may be a beneficial addition to your wardrobe, and working with a stylist will help you determine whether you'd better be served by something functional like a pair of rain boots or something fashionable like a peep-toe bootie.

Sneakers

For some women sneakers are strictly for yoga or tennis or other athletic pursuits, while for others they're a major part of their wardrobe. Whether you only wear them to sweat in or choose to make them a part of your regular shoe rotation is up to you. If you're wearing them to the gym, make sure that they're suited for the activities you're doing and not a dressed down fashion sneaker which will have no support. If they're primarily a fashion feature, though, you should try interesting shapes like wedges or on-trend color and fabric combinations to best complement the rest of your outfit.

Wedges

Like ballerina flats, wedges are incredibly versatile but they're not appropriate for every event or location. Wedge sandals can look amazing with a short summer weight dress at an outdoor event and they're wider base makes them more sturdy than other heeled sandals, but they often won't work in a traditional office or other more formal setting.

Pumps

Every woman needs to own at least one pair of pumps. In both black and neutral they're suitable for almost any situation. While in more vibrant shades like emerald green or with interesting textures such as suede or lace, they can be the best choice in footwear for a night out. However, because of the many variables like toe shapes, strap options and heel heights, the input of a stylist can be a major help.

Accessories

The "it" Bag. A bold bangle. The perfect sunglasses. All of these are little extras that are absolutely essential for any well-rounded wardrobe. And sometimes they're all you need to completely change a look. Similar to shoes, accessories are also available almost anywhere that you can buy clothes but sometimes a dedicated destination is the best option.

How to get the most from your experience: Unless you're shopping for something basic like a pair of small hoop earrings or a black clutch, it'll help immensely if you have a game plan. If you're trying to find a piece to match something that you already have in your wardrobe, it helps if you have the item with you. If that isn't possible, then the next best thing is a couple of clear pictures taken both in natural light and in light similar to where you'll be when your outfit is complete.

What to avoid: While it's great to have some amazing statement pieces that you can pair with more basic clothing for instant impact, don't buy a piece simply because it's unique. Consider if it's realistically something that you'd wear and what you could possibly pair it with. Conversely, don't solely stick to the most basic items that you can find, consider that something like a bold bag or stack of bangles can pair well with a basic black ensemble. Having a stylist with you can help in making these decisions.

Jewelry

You've likely heard the statement "Diamonds are a girl's best friend" but that doesn't even begin to cover the love affair that can come as the result of a well-stocked jewelry box. Whether the pieces you pick are meant to add just a touch of sparkle or are the star of the show, will ultimately be up to the outfit that you select and what you're trying to convey, but there are some do's and don'ts that you should keep in mind. For more in-depth information, a stylist can help you stock up on pieces that best match your personal means.

Do remain mindful of length. Whether you're looking at necklaces or long earrings you need to understand how they're going to lay. When looking at necklaces you want pieces that flatter the neckline of whatever you're wearing and note that if the piece has a pendant that most people will initially rest their eyes where it lays. When considering longer earrings, anything longer than shoulder length can be problematic, so you'll want to consider factors such as how you plan on wearing your hair and whether or not the shoulders of your top are embellished as embellishments can clash.

Don't buy pieces that are too heavy. No matter how drawn you are to a piece you have to retain a critical eye when it comes to whether or not the piece weighs you down. Items such as earrings that stretch your lobes are not items that you want to own.

Do incorporate a mix of classic and trendy pieces. Items such as a long strand of pearls, small gold hoops and cocktail rings are timeless and can be amazing go to items in a range of situations, but they shouldn't be the only pieces you own. Add a few trendy pieces to your jewelry selection as a means of keeping it current and giving it new energy.

Don't confuse having signature pieces with being in a styling rut. Over time you may realize that there are certain pieces of jewelry that you wear repeatedly, so much so that these pieces can be associated with you. Ask yourself if you really adore those items or if they're just what you've gotten used to pairing with certain outfits. If it's the latter, take the time to look through your jewelry box and see what else may work. If you find yourself stumped, a styling session could help you see things through someone else's eyes.

Bags

The right bag offers you one more chance to show off your personal style. Whether it's a bejeweled miniaudière that you've paired with a sleek evening gown and strapped stilettos for a charity event or a tote that you've paired with khaki shorts, flats and a fitted tee for a morning at the farmer's market, the right bag can be the perfect accompaniment while the wrong bag can ruin an outfit. Keep in mind that there's no single right bag or wrong bag, only what's right or wrong for the situation.

Handbags and shoulder bags come in a range of sizes from small to extra large. The one you select depends on where you're going and what you need to take with you. For instance, if you're going to work you'll want something small to medium-sized. As a general rule of thumb, you don't want a bag so large that it looks empty when you open it after you've put whatever you need inside, but you also don't want it to be so full that you can't find what you need without spending fifteen minutes emptying it out.

Tote bags can range from high-end luxury leather goods to canvas freebies, and both have their place. The former is great for a relaxed afternoon outdoors while the latter can be used for eco-friendly shopping.

Clutches range in sizes from extra small to large. Extra small ones are perfect for evenings out at the opera or other events where you want your bag to add to your outfit but not overwhelm it. Larger clutches can be perfect for date night or girl's night. Make sure, though, that your clutch is large enough to comfortably hold your essentials because you don't want your bag to have bulges.

Miscellaneous Items

There are certain additional elements which you may not be considering that can take a good outfit and make it great. While these pieces won't work with every outfit, when they're properly incorporated they can add an almost magical quality to your overall look.

Brooches

Sometimes a brooch is exactly what you need to add a bit of interest to an outfit that even when accessorized still looks a little flat. Consider unconventional placement such as on the breast pocket of a jacket so that it appears like a three dimensional crest, or add one to a headband for some additional sparkle.

Pocket squares

While pocket squares are a staple of menswear, there's nothing stopping a woman from incorporating them into her corporate attire for an extra pop of color.

Hats, headbands, turbans and fascinators

Headwear can be an amazing addition to an outfit. A turban looks chic when paired with a flowing caftan and jeweled sandals, while a veiled fascinator helps to complete a vintage-inspired look when paired with a wiggle dress and a pair of pumps.

Gloves

While gloves are certainly functional in cold weather, they can be fashionable at any time. For example, long satin gloves lend themselves well to evening wear.

Belts

A great belt can be a statement piece that requires very little effort. Consider wearing a brightly colored belt over your little black dress or adding a metallic belt to a monochromatic outfit.

Fur stoles

Whether real or faux, a fur stole helps add instant glamour to a look and looks equally amazing with a long or a short dress.

Tights

Tights can be textured or dip dyed, seamed or bejeweled. Even plain colored tights can have an amazing impact and take an outfit from "okay" to "outstanding."

All accessories act as a way of helping you best define your style and so you should have fun with it. Try on a few different pieces with the same outfit and be sure to give yourself options. If you realize that you need another opinion, a stylist is always a great option and will help you find what best suits you and your wardrobe.

Chapter 7: Saving vs. Splurging

"Fashion is not necessarily about labels. It's not about brands. It's about something that comes from within you." - Ralph Lauren

The price tag attached to an item doesn't determine the value it'll have in your wardrobe. Whether you spend $30.00 or $300.00 on a dress, it's real worth is determined by how often you wear it and how awesome you feel in it. Keeping that in mind there are certain things that you'll want to, and should spend significant money on but there are other things that you can save on. Every piece, whether it's a current Prada purse or no-name brand black t-shirt, is something that requires you to consider whether quality or quantity is more important. This compromise can get confusing, a small price tag doesn't always signal that something is sub-par, so if you're unsure it may be best to consult a stylist. What follows is a basic guide that takes into account what you may want in your closet and whether it's worth splurging on or if you should save your money and spend less.

Basics

The basic pieces in your wardrobe are the ones in your personal capsule collection. These are the pieces such as the "emergency dress" and your favorites jeans that were mentioned in chapter 1.

When to save: These pieces are the building blocks of your entire wardrobe and, therefore as a general rule, they should be the absolute best quality that you can find to complement your body type.

When to splurge: If you find something that you absolutely love the cut of, like a well fitting blazer, don't hesitate to buy it in a couple of colors. As these are timeless pieces, they'll always be in fashion so you can feel good about providing yourself with some options.

How to save: Unless you already have a brand you love for t-shirts, silk blouses or cashmere cardigans, try the company Everlane (https://www.everlane.com/) for pieces that are both affordable and well made.

Evening wear

From cocktail dresses to ball gowns, evening wear has been around for centuries in some form or another. You may attend one charity function every few months or have a social calendar that's completely full of galas. Your particular need for this type of clothing is going to determine how you go about procuring it.

When to save: If you're a woman who spends every weekend or even every other weekend in sequins, silks or satins then you may think that you need a closet specifically for your formal wear, and while this isn't necessarily wrong, it isn't entirely right either. What you need isn't a specific wardrobe for these functions, what you need are options and you can have thousands of them without spending millions of dollars.

When to splurge: Is it your first time at the Opera or at a museum gala or masquerade ball? If so, then chances are good you want to stand out and feel particularly special. These are the occasions where you may want to splurge on something particularly show-stopping that you can make entirely your own.

How to save: Featuring designers such as Halston Heritage, Carmen Marc Valvo and Reem Acra, Rent the Runway (www.renttherunway.com) offers incredible dress rentals for a fraction of the price you'd pay retail. This makes them an amazing option for someone who has a lot of commitments requiring evening wear but is looking to save retail space in their closets for pieces that are more functional, and isn't willing to compromise quality for the option of quantity.

Shoes

There are so many different options that exist in terms of shoes, from sleek stilettos that are perfect for power lunches to cute flats for tooling around town in. It can be incredibly tempting to buy every pair that we have even a passing fancy for but all that's likely to do is clutter our closets.

When to save: When you come across a pair of shoes that you love that isn't entirely conducive to your lifestyle or that'll go with exactly one or two things in your wardrobe, that isn't the pair that you should be spending thousands of dollars on. This logic should also be applied to shoes you have to buy, such as a pair that's meant to match a bridesmaids dress or ones that are incredibly trendy.

When to splurge: Just like the clothing in your capsule wardrobe, the shoes that serve as foundational should be the ones that you spend the most money on as they're the ones which will likely be worn the most frequently.

How to save: Stay away from untrusted/unvouched for Internet sites such as those that claim to sell Louboutin heels for only $100, and instead look in reputable consigner stores for gently worn shoes or try smaller boutiques for indie brands to get your fix for shoes that may not be fashionable for more than a season or so.

Bags

Our bags can, in many ways, be as important as what we put in them. Whether it's the tote that we take with us on vacation or the handbag we carry on a daily basis, the right bag can make or break an outfit, and so it's important that both quality and quantity are addressed.

When to save: The ornate minaudiere you want for a cocktail party doesn't need to be Alexander McQueen to make a statement, especially if you only plan on using it for one night. The same is true for any bags that are trendy and which you won't really incorporate into your wardrobe past a season, these are not the bags that you need to spend thousands of dollars on.

When to splurge: Iconic bags, such as the quilted Chanel purse with the chain strap, will always be stylish and as such those pieces are the ones you should be willing to spend more on. Also, any bag that you could literally utilize everyday is one that you want to be sure has great quality.

How to save: Bag, Borrow or Steal (http://www.bagborroworsteal.com/) allows you to rent designer bags by the month for trendy pieces or you can check out the private sales section of their website for heavily discounted pre-owned pieces.

Accessories

Accessories serve as a huge part of pulling an outfit together. Whether it's a bold belt to add a pop of color or an amazing cocktail ring, there's just something amazing about the way that those pieces serve to create finishing touches that help showcase your style.

When to save: Most accessories can be purchased inexpensively and they should be if you want to ensure that you have a wide array of options. Don't shy away from sites that specialize in trendy pieces or stores that cater to a more junior audience for awesome costume pieces.

When to splurge: Diamond studs, a strand of pearls, the perfect watch; these are all pieces that it's okay to spend more money on because they're eternally chic and will always serve you well.

How to save: Emitations (http://www.emitations.com) offers an incredible selection of high-end looking pieces at prices that are incredibly reasonable.

Whether you're saving or splurging, or if you're unsure of what to do, a stylist can help to ensure that you're getting the best for both your body type and your budget.

Chapter 8: Who. What. Wear. Pt. 1

"Playing dress-up begins at age five and never truly ends." - Kate Spade

Answering the question of what to wear isn't always an easy one, even when you have a closet full of amazing pieces to put together. There also isn't just one perfect outfit that makes sense for a particular occasion and somehow knowing that can make the process of picking something out to wear even more overwhelming. Consider what follows a cheat sheet, a guide that looks at some of life's more common events, considers your capsule wardrobe, and helps you create stellar looks at any age and with any body type.

First Impressions

The old adage is true, we're never given a second chance to make a first impression and, as such, it's important that when given the opportunity to present ourselves for the first time that we do so in a way that helps show how fabulous we are and style plays a big role in doing that.

Job Interview

Whether you're interviewing for the first time or for the hundredth, interviews can be especially nerve-wracking. You need to be focused both on how you look and how you're presenting yourself. Keep in mind that the below tips are for a job in a corporate setting, if you're interviewing at some place that is more relaxed or artistic, consult with a stylist for the best course of action.

From your capsule wardrobe: blazer, black Louboutin pumps, a classic handbag and a crisp white button-down. When combined, these pieces help to create an overall look that's polished and powerful.

In your **20s**: Add a coordinating skirt that falls just below knee length and stick with a more classic corporate color palette, such as a plain navy blazer with a navy pinstripe skirt. You want to convey a sense of style without wearing anything that can be immediately identified as being trendy or junior.

In your **30s**: Add a coordinating skirt that falls just above or just below your knee. Don't feel the need to match the pieces in terms of color but keep the colors classic. For example, a red blazer paired with a black skirt looks both sophisticated and interesting.

In your **40s**: Add a coordinating skirt that falls just below knee length or fitted pair of trousers. Opt for colors like a light gray, navy or red, and try to add a bit of texture either with a supple leather blazer or a silk scarf on your handbag.

In your **50s**: Omit the white button-up and wear a sheath dress under your blazer. It's a bit of a bolder move in an interview setting and will make you much more memorable. Either opt for a black blazer and a colored dress or vice versa.

If you're a **triangle** body type: Draw the interest to the top of your body with a blazer in a great color, subtle print or one with a bit of texture.

If you're an **inverted triangle** body type: Utilize darker colors on the top e.g. a black or navy blazer and draw interest on your ensemble as a whole or opting for a skirt or trousers with a bit of flare.

If you're a **rectangle** body type: Add a belt to the look in order to create a more proportional look.

If you're a **diamond** body type: Opt for a look where the skirt is the focal point, additionally be sure to wear the blazer open.

If you're an **apple** body type: To create the best proportions fit is key, make sure that both the blazer and the skirt create flattering lines and avoid a belt or anything with belt loops.

If you're an **hourglass** body type: Make sure that the fit of all of your pieces flatters your curves as opposed to flaunting them and opt for items in complementary color families.

First date

You may be going out with someone you know from school or work or someone you just met in the gym, either way the focus should be on having a nice time and not stressing about what you're going to wear. Keep in mind you want to wear something that will make you feel confident.

From your capsule wardrobe: Black or nude pumps and your perfect accessory. This isn't the time to break in a pair of new shoes and having something both familiar and fabulous like your signature accessory will help pull together any outfit.

In your **20s**: add a mini skirt, or skirt right above the knee with a coordinating silk top.

In your **30s**: add a dark wash of fitted jeans and a silk cami and pair it with your basic blazer. Don't be afraid to cuff the blazer to give it a more fun appeal opposed to a corporate feel.

In your **40s**: add a knee-length pin skirt in a color appropriate to the season and coordinating blouse with your perfect accessory.

In your **50s**: Add fitted black pants and a silk blouse paired with your black or nude pumps.

If you're a **triangle** body type: Make your top the emphasis of your outfit by opting for something in a color that you adore or a flattering fabric.

If you're an **inverted triangle** body type: Opt for a look where the bottom piece is the one with the majority of interest. Don't feel the need to be flashy, per se, and instead focus on fabrics that are texturally interesting but still comfortable.

If you're a **rectangle** body type: Decide whether you want to play up your naturally more athletic shape or create the illusion of greater curves. I suggest doing the former by selecting pieces that are cut to flatter your figure.

If you're a **diamond** body type: Keep the selected pieces form-fitting, but not tight, and play up what you consider your personal best assets to be.

If you're an **apple** body type: Keep your mind on colors and select those that you feel most comfortable in.

If you're an **hourglass** body type: Resist the urge to overemphasize your curves and instead select pieces that, while form-fitting, don't expose too much skin.

First time meeting the parents/family of your significant other

This is one of those cases where you definitely want to keep your wardrobe more conservative. This doesn't mean that your look can't have some personality, it should. But it should also be something that will be palatable for almost anyone. No matter how open-minded you've been told these people are, now isn't the time for super wild prints, cut-offs or cut outs.

From your capsule wardrobe: Your cashmere cardigan or duster and ballet flats. Both of these are classy pieces that are also casual.

In your **20s**: Add a blouse with a simple print and a pair of skinny jeans. If the meeting is meant to be a more dressed-up occasion swap a knee length skirt for the jeans and your black or nude pumps for your flats.

In your **30s**: Add your emergency dress and swap out your black or nude pumps for your flats.

In your **40s**: Add a pin skirt and a blouse.

In your **50s**: Add a sheath dress and a strand of pearls. Swap out your black or nude pumps for your flats.

If you're a **triangle** body type: If you're wearing separates, select a blouse that has an interesting but non distracting print e.g. small polka dots. If your plus-sized, skip the print and instead select a blouse in a luxurious looking shade like camel or steel gray. If you're wearing a dress, select one with a square or rounded neckline that isn't too low.

If you're an **inverted triangle** body type: Utilize darker colors up top with lighter ones near the bottom of your look. In creating your own ombre effect you help to give your look greater balance.

If you're a **rectangle** body type: Incorporate a belt or a sash to give your waist a more defined look.

If you're a **diamond** body type: Select fabrics that have a natural flow to them e.g. an opaque chiffon blouse or a dress made from jersey material.

If you're an **apple** body type: Look for pieces that have a bit of stretch and also try to select more natural fabrics like silks and cottons.

If you're an **hourglass** body type: Be very mindful of proportions, and if possible, opt for something with a higher neckline or lower hemline.

New Year's Eve

Arguably the glitziest night of the year, New Year's Eve is a time for you to shine, and since whatever you're wearing on December 31st will ultimately be your first outfit of the new year, it should be something stunning.

From your capsule wardrobe: Your black or nude pumps. Just like for a first date, this is not the best time to break in new shoes.

In your **20s**: Opt for a look that's both fun and functional such by adding a sequin mini-dress with tights and a wristlet.

In your **30s**: Add a cocktail dress with embellishments and a leather jacket along with sheer hose, an oversized clutch and a cocktail ring.

In your **40s**: Add a sheer blouse, a sequin blazer and a pair of leather or waxed-denim pants.

In your **50s**: Add a sheath dress along with a jeweled brooch and sheer panty hose with a fur (faux or real) coat and an evening bag.

If you're a **triangle** body type: Opt for pops of color and beading near your shoulders, neckline or bust line.

If you're an **inverted triangle** body type: Look for a skirt or pants that have a bit of a flare.

If you're a **rectangle** body type: Let your top or your dress act as the focal point of your outfit.

If you're a **diamond** body type: Avoid anything high-waisted or too tight. Also, stay away from fabrics with no stretch.

If you're an **apple** body type: Look for a dress or top with an interesting neckline and select fabrics that hug but don't constrict your form.

If you're an **hourglass** body type: Select something in a rich hue that has details and embellishments that appeal to you but don't overwhelm the look.

Traveling

Just the thought of a long flight is enough to make some people anxious, and that anxiety shouldn't extend to what you're going to wear in order to be comfortable for hours both at the airport and on the airplane.

Commercial flight

Flying commercial means needing to conform to the regulations of airport security and that doesn't exactly conjure images of style icons. It is, however, possible to be both comfortable and able to quickly clear any checkpoints.

From your capsule wardrobe: Your classic handbag and ballet flats. Your handbag, if properly sized, is the perfect carry-on bag for anything you're taking on your trip that you don't want to check, like a particular pair of earrings or your favorite heels, and ballet flats slip on and off effortlessly.

In your **20s**: Add leggings and a tunic top. Keep the colors dark e.g. black or gray for a more sophisticated overall look.

In your **30s**: Add your cashmere cardigan or duster and a knee length Jersey dress for a look that'll take you from the airport to lunch or dinner at your hotel with ease.

In your **40s**: wear your favorite jeans (best if they have some stretch), a white tee and add a pashmina wrap.

In your **50s**: add a breathable cotton dress in a dark color that you could throw your basic blazer or cashmere duster over.

If you're a **triangle** body type: Feel free to opt for a top with some texture or in a bold color to create a greater sense of balance. If you're wearing a dress, seek out something with an interesting neck line.

If you're an **inverted triangle** body type: Don't feel the need to shy away from leggings or pants that have tone on tone patterns or a jersey dress with a print near the bottom to draw the eye downward.

If you're a **rectangle** body type: Now is great time to opt for roomier pieces. While you don't want fabrics that overwhelm your frame, it's okay if they hang a little looser than the pieces you'd normally wear.

If you're a **diamond** body type: Select a look that doesn't require a belt and is fairly form fitting.

If you're an **apple** body type: Opt for a look that is either fairly monochromatic in either a black or gray and include a pop of color in your shoes.

If you're an **hourglass** body type: Feel free to wear a patterned dress or patterned leggings. Just ensure that your duster, wrap or top is in a complimentary color.

Private flight

Flying on a private plane often means many wonderful things like not worrying about your luggage being lost, more leg room and the ability to wear something that will look amazing anywhere and isn't just suitable for the airport.

From your capsule wardrobe: Cashmere cardigan or duster and a classic handbag. The cardigan or duster will give you some added comfort while the handbag offers convenience both on and off the plane.

In your **20s**: Add your favorite jeans, a crisp white tee and your black pumps. The overall effect is a look that's sophisticated and eternally on trend.

In your **30s**: Add skinny stretchy jeans, or, if you're daring a cargo pant. They are great for traveling with the extra pockets and a basic white tee with your cashmere duster.

In your **40s**: Add a maxi dress. This can be comfortable and look fabulous so you're ready to go when you arrive. Pair it with wedges or booties depending on the destination.

In your **50s**: Add a jersey dress, they are great for traveling and wrinkle resistant. Pair it with flats or pumps.

If you're a **triangle** body type: Select something that has an interesting neckline and allow the rest of your outfit to be more toned down in terms of pattern and color.

If you're an **inverted triangle** body type: When wearing separates, look for a bottom that is interesting e.g. a printed or patterned jean or silk cargo pants. When wearing a dress select something that's color-blocked.

If you're a **rectangle** body type: Decide whether you want a look that is loose and boxy or something more form-fitting. For a boxier look with separates, select a tunic or hi-lo top and for the same look with a dress select a t-shirt style dress. For a more fitted look utilize a belt or a sash.

If you're a **diamond** body type: Select fabrics that are a bit looser but not baggy. If you're wearing skinny jeans opt for a top that falls about a 1/2 inch to 1 inch below your waistline.

If you're an **apple** body type: Make sure that whatever you select is form fitting but not tight, and any embellishments should be away from your midriff.

If you're an **hourglass** body type: Feel free to add a shirt with a pattern or jeans in a vibrant color. Just make sure that everything coordinates.

Shopping

It may not immediately seem as if you need a specific option for shopping, but you do. You want to make sure that what you're wearing is comfortable and that, if necessary (like at a sample sale), you can slip in and out of it easily. Additionally, keep in mind what you're shopping for and if it's something that you'll be wearing your shapewear with, make sure that you have your shapewear on so that you know exactly what the outfit will look like as opposed to just having an idea of what it might look like.

From your capsule wardrobe: Your ballet flats and handbag. You want shoes that aren't likely to hurt your feet and a handbag that's cross-body and not small enough that if you put it down it could be easily forgotten.

In your **20s**: Add leggings and a long fitted tee in dark tones for a look that's effortless and easy to maneuver in.

In your **30s**: Add a Jersey dress for something that doesn't wrinkle or bunch, and which you'll be able to slip in and out if.

In your **40s**: Add a pair of drawstring pants in either silk or cotton with a basic white tee and ballet flats.

In your **50s**: Add a pair of jeans with stretch in them, wear them with a cotton tee and your cashmere cardigan and ballet flats.

If you're a **triangle** body type: Since you'll want to avoid necklaces or hoop earrings to avoid potential snagging, opt for a patterned top (small prints if you're petite, bolder ones if your plus size).

If you're an **inverted triangle** body type: If you're wearing separates color is key, select a rich shade for your pants such as navy or olive. If you're wearing a dress, try something with a print on the bottom or color blocking.

If you're a **rectangle** body type: Now is a good time to show off your shape as it naturally, is so opt for pieces that are form-fitting but not tight.

If you're a **diamond** body type: Look for pieces that stretch and are loose enough that they don't bunch, wear a darker colored top with a lighter colored bottom.

If you're an **apple** body type: You want to make sure that whatever you have on is loose, but not baggy or boxy around the midriff.

If you're an **hourglass** body type: Keep the look simple and free of embellishments. If you'd like something more dressed up, opt for a print or a bold color as a way of enhancing the look.

Parties

Parties offer a great chance for you to connect and network, and while you may be worried about things like an appropriate gift for the hostess you should never be worried about what you're going to wear.

A dinner party you're hosting

When you're the hostess you have the right to feel especially glamorous, so don't shy away from dressing up. If you're cooking, as opposed to ordering in take-out or having the event catered, be sure to top your look with an apron while you're in the kitchen.

From your capsule wardrobe: Your black Louboutin pumps and a piece of statement jewelry. These are both strong pieces that command attention and help keep your look center stage.

In your **20s**: Add a black silk or satin jumpsuit or romper.

In your **30s**: Add a silk or sheer t-shirt in a bold color with black tuxedo style pants.

In your **40s**: Add a silk or satin short kimono in a vibrant pattern or print worn open over a shell top, and pair it with jeans.

In your **50s**: Add a sheath dress in a jewel tone.

If you're a **triangle** body type: Highlight your bust with a daring neckline and opt for a look where the bottom is sleek as opposed to voluminous.

If you're an **inverted triangle** body type: Look for a way to make your pants or the bottom of your skirt the focal point. In both cases a jeweled hem adds a bit of interest without going overboard.

If you're a **rectangle** body type: Consider ways to cinch in or draw attention to your waist. If you're wearing a jumpsuit, romper or dress, try a wide obi style belt, for all other looks a belt in a bold color will work.

If you're a **diamond** body type: Look for pieces that are slightly looser up top for a more bloused effect. Avoid anything baggy or boxy.

If you're an **apple** body type: Stay away from fabrics that are stiff, if possible look for pieces that incorporate some stretch.

If you're an **hourglass** body type: Find ways to incorporate an interesting color into your look and be mindful that your neckline isn't too low on your top.

A dinner party you're attending

In addition to a host or hostess gift, also bring your sense of style with a look that's equal parts sophisticated and comfortable. Keep in mind that the person holding the dinner may have distinct ideas about attire so it's best to inquire beforehand, but in the event that the event is semi-formal the looks below will look perfect.

From your capsule wardrobe: Your ballet flats. These are a comfortable shoe that will add a bit of polish without making you look overdressed.

In your **20s**: Add your cashmere cardigan or duster, a silk tank top and leather leggings (faux or real)

In your **30s**: Swap out your ballet flats for your black or nude pumps and add a tea length skirt and a silk tank or t-shirt.

In your **40s**: Add jeans, a sleeveless chiffon blouse and your cashmere cardigan or duster.

In your **50s**: Add a cigarette length pant, a sleeveless or short sleeved blouse and your blazer.

If you're a **triangle** body type: Look for a top with interesting elements, this may include a particularly pretty texture or pattern, or if you're particularly daring, something with cut-out shoulders or a cut-out back.

If you're an **inverted triangle** body type: Opt for a bottom in a bold or unexpected color. Consider gray as opposed to black leather leggings, jeans in pastel or primary colors or a patterned skirt or cigarette pants.

If you're a **rectangle** body type: If you want to accent your shape look for pieces that are form-fitting. If you want to create a different shape, focus on your waist area by incorporating a wide or patterned belt.

If you're a **diamond** body type: opt for a lower neckline and an interesting hemline.

If you're an **apple** body type: Avoid fabrics that are stiff or clingy.

If you're an **hourglass** body type: Try to find a top with some movement and keep your bottom form-fitting.

An office party

No matter how casual the setting, an office party is still ultimately a professional event and so you need to ensure that your outfit is stylish but more modest than it would be for other occasions.

From your capsule wardrobe: Black pumps. Despite being super stylish, these shoes are also "safe" and should be the inspiration for the rest of your look.

In your **20s**: Add a little black dress that falls slightly below your knee, a boldly-colored or patterned blazer for a bit of interest and a clutch. Keep jewelry minimal with a great statement necklace or a pair of earrings.

In your **30s**: Add your emergency dress and cashmere cardigan or duster.

In your **40s**: Add well-tailored tuxedo style pants and add your crisp button-up shirt.

In your **50s**: Add a wrap or a shift dress for an effortless look that is professional, timeless and appropriate.

If you're a **triangle** body type: Allow your accessories to highlight your neckline as opposed to opting for a piece of clothing that may be too low cut, and ensure that the darkest elements of your outfit are on the bottom. Avoid any hemline that doesn't sit at slightly below your knee or lower.

If you're an **inverted triangle** body type. Opt for darker hues especially near your top and avoid wearing a statement necklace, opting for simple bangles or a tennis bracelet instead.

If you're a **rectangle** body type: Now is a great time to highlight your shape with looser fitting but still tailored options.

If you're a **diamond** body type: Select fabrics like jersey and cotton for a look that's chic and will move with you.

If you're an **apple** body type: Incorporate a mix of darker and lighter colors into your look, with the darker ones being concentrated in your midsection area.

If you're an **hourglass** body type: Utilize fabrics with beautiful drape that won't hug your curves. You want to look more sophisticated than sexy.

Your engagement party

Congrats on your upcoming wedding! Let your new bling act as the perfect accent to your outfit. That, plus the smile on your face, will make sure that your look is especially memorable.

From your capsule wardrobe: This is one of the rare occasions when an entirely new look is in order. Instead of a piece or two from your capsule collection, let's consider this a practice run for the big day and get you decked out in white which can be worn various ways.

In your **20s**: Opt for a white or ivory romper or jumpsuit, and a pair of jeweled or boldly colored stilettos.

In your **30s**: Opt for a cocktail length white, ivory or cream dress. Accent the look with a pair of boldly colored or patterned stilettos.

In your **40s**: Opt for white skinny pants, an embellished silk blouse in a pale hue and a pair of jeweled stilettos.

In your **50s**: Opt for a white or champagne pantsuit with a lace or beaded cami in the same color and silver (if you're wearing white) or gold (if you're wearing champagne) sandals, kitten heels or flats.

If you're a **triangle** body type: Make your neckline or your shoulders the area of interest. This can be done with an asymmetry, beading or shoulder pads.

If you're an **inverted triangle** body type: Go for a look where the primary area of interest is at or below your waist. If you're in a romper, jumpsuit or pantsuit, opt for something with flared legs. If you're wearing skinny pants try and find one with a pattern or a lace overlay, and in a cocktail dress consider a drop waist style or something with fringe.

If you're a **rectangle** body type: Look for a jeweled, patterned or colorful belt to pair with your look.

If you're a **diamond** body type: Select a look where the top has more flow than the bottom, you don't want something boxy but you don't want something with movement.

If you're an **apple** body type: Ensure that whatever you select isn't overly tight or embellished near your midriff, instead make sure that your assets are what's highlighted.

If you're an **hourglass** body type: Keep your look simple and minimally embellished, you want to make sure that your proportions stay balanced.

An engagement party you're attending

The only rule to really follow is to not upstage the bride-to-be. This means keeping your look toned down. You can and should look chic but not in a way that upstages the woman of the hour. Keep in mind that, as there's no right way to announce an engagement, the couple may choose to do something incredibly casual, something white-tie or anything in between. Before selecting your exact outfit be sure to inquire. If the event is semi-formal the following will be perfect. If not and you're unsure what to wear, be sure to contact a stylist.

From your capsule wardrobe: Your oversized clutch and your black Louboutin heels. You want to make sure that you have enough room for all of your essentials and great shoes that will be the basis for a great outfit that isn't overly flashy.

In your **20s**: Add a skater dress and a cocktail ring.

In your **30s**: Add a cocktail dress and a tennis bracelet or small hoop earrings.

In your **40s**: Add a wrap dress and a statement accessory.

In your **50s**: Add a knee length sheath dress and your pearls or cocktail ring along with a Pashmina wrap if the weather is cool.

If you're a **triangle** body type: In a skater, cocktail or sheath dress, look for something with an interesting back or a cutout. For a wrap dress, opt for something longer and in a dark hue.

If you're an **inverted triangle** body type: Look for something with color blocking where the darker colors are near the top.

If you're a **rectangle** body type: Show off your shape with something that has an interesting texture or fabric. If you're looking to create the illusion of a more proportioned figure, cinch your waist with a jeweled belt or sash.

If you're a **diamond** body type: Find a dress that is well fitting but that does not hug your midsection.

If you're an **apple** body type: Look for something that has a bold all over print.

If you're an **hourglass** body type: Opt for something in a darker hue and make sure that your dress is at least knee length with a scoop, square or demure v-neck line.

Your bachelorette party

Whether it's the night before your wedding or a weekend event that happens the week before, your bachelorette party is a great time to get dressed up and spend some time with your bridal party and best girlfriends. You may be planning a day/night full of fun events and so what follows is a more "traditional" blueprint for getting dressed. If you're doing something more specific, contact a stylist.

From your capsule wardrobe: Similar to your engagement party, this is another occasion when you can pick out a whole new look.

In your **20s**: Opt for a sequin or print mini-dress with bold colored or nude pumps, an oversized clutch and stud, hoop or chandelier earrings based on your preferences.

In your **30s**: Opt for a jersey dress, a jeweled clutch and metallic or nude stilettos.

In your **40s**: Opt for tuxedo or metallic colored pants, a black tank, a fitted black blazer, black stilettos, an evening bag and a statement necklace.

In your **50s**: Opt for a little black dress or a little white dress as per your preferences, a Pashima wrap in a bold color, black pumps and an oversized clutch.

If you're a **triangle** body type: Look for sweetheart necklines to help highlight your shoulders.

If you're an **inverted triangle** body type: Opt for lighter colors on the bottom, e.g. dresses with color blocking or ombre that fades to a light color, or tuxedo pants in a classic hue like white.

If you're a **rectangle** body type: Celebrate your shape in something that's form-fitting.

If you're a **diamond** body type: Wear a dress in a dark hue with a coordinating wide belt or sash. If you're wearing pants, opt for a white tank and fitted white blazer with dark tuxedo or metallic colored pants.

If you're an **apple** body type: Look for a bold print that can be incorporated into the look, either in an overall print on the dress or on the blazer.

If you're an **hourglass** body type: In your 30s, opt for a bandage style dress to really showcase your shape. In every other age group look for pieces that flatter your figure and make you feel sexy.

A bachelorette party you're attending

Similar to attendance at someone else's engagement party, the rule here is to let the bride-to-be, be the center of attention. Keep in mind that the bride to be may have her own ideas about dress code and so she should be consulted first. Consider that she may want all attendees in a certain color, a certain style of dress or even in an outfit that fits a theme. Call her before you call a stylist. In the event that she's looking to something that's casual, like bar hopping or an evening at a lounge, the following looks should serve you well.

From your capsule wardrobe: Select your nude pumps and oversized clutch. These are great starter pieces to build the rest of your look around because while they're certainly classic they also pair well with trendier pieces.

In your **20s**: Add a pair of printed or colored jeans and a basic silk tee or tank.

In your **30s**: Add a sequin top with skinny jeans and a pair of earrings.

In your **40s**: Add leather leggings and a tunic top with a necklace.

In your **50s**: Add a pair of cigarette length pants and a blouse along with your cocktail ring.

If you're a **triangle** body type: Look for a top that's either asymmetrical or one with an interesting neckline.

If you're an **inverted triangle** body type: Opt for a darker-hued top. Look for luxurious colors like wine, chocolate and camel.

If you're a **rectangle** body type: Look for a top in an interesting fabric, such as leather or chiffon.

If you're a **diamond** body type: Opt for a lighter colored top with an interesting neckline or sleeves, and pair it with a darker bottom.

If you're an **apple** body type: Look for softer, non-clingy materials for your top and make sure your pants are well-fitting.

If you're an **hourglass** body type: Opt for a more monochromatic look by selecting various shades of the same color. This looks especially good on all skin tones with neutral/cream, black or gray.

Your birthday party

It's your birthday and a chance to truly stand out as the stylish woman you are. Select something memorable.

From your capsule wardrobe: Select your Black Louboutin's and know that you're stepping into the next year in style.

In your **20s**: Add a sequin skirt with a silk tank top and a leather jacket and bold colored clutch.

In your **30s**: Add a vibrant-colored print dress and a jeweled clutch.

In your **40s**: Add a cocktail dress, an evening bag and a statement accessory.

In your **50s**: Add a red dress, your cocktail ring and a jeweled clutch.

If you're a **triangle** body type: Add a bold necklace to your look and look for a skirt or dress with a longer length.

If you're an **inverted triangle** body type: Look for something that is plain near the top. If you're wearing a tank top make sure that it isn't embellished. If you're wearing a dress, opt for a square or high neckline.

If you're a **rectangle** body type: Select pieces that are slightly boxy to highlight your shape or cinch your waist.

If you're a **diamond** body type: Look for darker colors that are still rich like emerald green and navy blue.

If you're an **apple** body type: Highlight your best asset as you see fit, this may mean showing off toned arms, shapely legs or a bit of cleavage.

If you're an **hourglass** body type: Look for a top that has a moderate to low v-neck and make sure that your skirt is no longer than knee length.

An adult birthday party you're attending

Adult parties can be as varied as those thrown for children and can include strict dress codes based on things such as theme, primary activity or even locale. If you're invited to a party that has a particular vibe the host or hostess is going for, be sure to respect that and call in a stylist if you find yourself stumped. For a more casual event, though, there are some basic looks you can't really go wrong with.

From your capsule wardrobe: Your crisp white tee or button up and nude pumps. These pieces will get slightly dressed up for a look that while casual is still totally chic.

In your **20s**: Utilize your white tee and add a pair of boyfriend-style jeans and a bold colored handbag.

In your **30s**: Utilize your white tee and add your blazer and a pair of skinny jeans with a coordinating handbag.

In your **40s**: Utilize your white button-up and add a pair or silk or satin trousers with an oversized clutch.

In your **50s**: Utilize your white tee and add a knee-length skirt.

If you're a **triangle** body type: Add statement earrings and opt for a dark bottom.

If you're an **inverted triangle** body type: Look for a bottom with a subtle print or texture or opt for a bottom in a bold color.

If you're a **rectangle** body type: Incorporate a long necklace and a few bangle bracelets to add interesting elements to your look.

If you're a **diamond** body type: Look for a dark bottom that, while fitted, isn't too tight and draw the eye to your neckline with a great necklace that complements the neckline or statement earrings.

If you're an **apple** body type: Opt for pieces that aren't loose or boxy and instead select pieces that fit well.

If you're an **hourglass** body type: Select pieces that show off your silhouette without being tight.

A child's birthday party that you're attending

Children's birthday parties can range from super casual events at a local park or beach, to larger-than-life lavish affairs in hotel ballrooms, based on everything from the age of the child to the general theme. As with any other event, check with your host for information regarding what's appropriate, and what follows is a look that will work in a more casual setting.

From your capsule wardrobe: Your ballet flats will be your best friend at a child's birthday party where there's likely to be at least a little running around. These shoes will inform the rest of your outfit, which while laid back, can still be fashion forward.

In your **20s**: Add your white tee and your favorite jeans.

In your **30s**: Add your favorite jeans and your cashmere cardigan or duster with a tank top.

In your **40s**: Add your favorite jeans and a bold colored tee.

In your **50s**: Add a pair of printed trousers and a shell top.

If you're a **triangle** body type: Select bottoms that are a dark hue but in a shade that coordinates with your ballet flats.

If you're an **inverted triangle** body type: Look for bottoms that have an interesting color or pattern. If you're wearing your favorite jeans, select a ballet flat that's printed.

If you're a **rectangle** body type: Keep your clothing fitted but not tight, and accentuate your waist with a boldly colored belt.

If you're a **diamond** body type: Incorporate a blazer or cardigan in your look in a color that coordinates with your flats for the most proportional look.

If you're an **apple** body type: Select a bottom that is slightly more fitted than your top and opt for patterns or colors that are particularly vibrant.

If you're an **hourglass** body type: Select a top with a slightly higher neckline than you'd normally incorporate and opt for a slightly boxier fitting bottom.

Beach Party

Regardless of who's throwing the party on the beach or the occasion, there are certain outfits that will always be perfect for the more casual event. If your host is putting together a more dressed up affair, contact a stylist to select something more appropriate.

From your capsule wardrobe: Your sunglasses, wide-brimmed hat and sunscreen are always going to be at home on the beach. Pair these pieces with easy fabrics and shapes for a look that's both effortless and elegant.

In your **20s**: Add a bold colored shirt-dress and gladiator sandals.

In your **30s**: Add a knee-length or shorter linen dress and sandals.

In your **40s**: Add a tee shirt-dress and espadrilles.

In your **50s**: Add a short caftan and jeweled sandals.

If you're a **triangle** body type: Select a dress with an interesting neckline or with an embellished collar.

If you're an **inverted triangle** body type: Look for a dress with a shorter length to emphasize your legs.

If you're a **rectangle** body type: Add a loose sash or thin belt to your waist for a pop of color and to create better proportions.

If you're a **diamond** body type: Select a dress in a darker hue and look for one with a hi-lo or flared skirt.

If you're an **apple** body type: Find a dress that is figure-flattering and neither too loose or too tight. Also, if looking for shirt-dresses or caftans, select natural fabrics like cottons or silks.

If you're an **hourglass** body type: Opt for a dress or caftan in a bold color to showcase your curves.

Miscellaneous occurrences

From an impromptu barbecue to weekly girls night out, there are a bevy of events that come up and all of them require a certain type of look.

A sporting event

Whether you're an avid fan, on a date or only in attendance to support a friend or family member, sporting events tend to be casual events. This doesn't mean that you can't be stylish as well.

From your capsule wardrobe: Let your favorite jeans serve as the building block for a look that's fashionable without being out of place.

In your **20s**: Add a team jersey and a pair of wedge sneakers in a coordinating color. Make sure that the jersey you select is one that's especially made for women.

In your **30s**: Add a tee shirt incorporating at least one of the team colors and a pair of ballet flats.

In your **40s**: Add a tank top in the team colors and a coordinating cardigan along with ballet flats.

In your **50s**: Add a shell top with at least one of the team colors and a pair of ballet flats.

If you're a **triangle** body type: Look for a top that's off the shoulder or one that has an interesting neckline.

If you're an **inverted triangle** body type: Select the darkest of the team colors to spotlight in your top.

If you're a **rectangle** body type: Select a top that sits exactly at the waist which will allow you to incorporate a belt in one of the team colors.

If you're a **diamond** body type: In lieu of a jersey, select a tee shirt with the team logo on it for a fit you have more control over. Make sure that any top you wear falls just slightly below your waist.

If you're an **apple** body type: Look for tops that have a deep v-neck line and ones that are looser around the midsection.

If you're an **hourglass** body type: Select the team color that's closest in terms of color to the wash of your jeans e.g. if your jeans are a dark wash select the darker of the team colors.

Indoor concert

The main benefits of an indoor concert as they pertain to your wardrobe is that there's generally some sort of temperature control, which means that you don't need to worry about layering your look and can instead look for an outfit that's ultimately most flattering to you. It may be tempting to simply pair a concert tee with jeans but it's much more fun and more fashion forward to create a look that has a lot more energy and personality, after all, this could be your chance to end up backstage meeting the band and if that's the case you want to be sure that your outfit hits all the right notes.

From your capsule wardrobe: Select your oversized clutch and if it came with a strap or a handle, now is the time to make sure you have it. This piece is perfect because it's small enough that it's not a burden and big enough that it's unlikely you'll lose it. Also, if you have box seats, as opposed to stadium seats, you'll also want your black Louboutins.

In your **20s**: Add moto pants in leather or a cotton blend, a bustier top and nude or black pumps.

In your **30s**: Add leather leggings or skinny jeans, a sheer blouse with a solid colored camisole underneath and bold or printed ballet flats.

In your **40s**: Add your favorite jeans, a tank top and bold colored ballet flats.

In your **50s**: Add your favorite jeans, a silk top and ballet flats or kitten heels.

If you're a **triangle** body type: Ignore necklaces and consider necklines. Opt for something that's different than what you'd normally wear and don't be afraid to show off some skin.

If you're an **inverted triangle** body type: Look for bottoms or shoes in interesting colors to draw the eye downward.

If you're a **rectangle** body type: Opt for a waist-length shirt or if you're wearing a bustier, look for one that's cropped and add your cardigan.

If you're a **diamond** body type: Pair your pants with a top that's lighter and carry the color from your top half down to your shoes for greater symmetry.

If you're an **apple** body type: Look for bold prints and interesting necklines for your top and keep your bottom form-fitting, but not tight.

If you're an **hourglass** body type: Look for pieces that highlight your curves but aren't too tight.

Outdoor concert

Outdoor concerts present unique styling challenges in that you want to be dressed appropriately for both the event and the weather without having too many extra pieces that could potentially be left behind. In a perfect world, every outdoor concert would take place on a mild summer day with clear skies and a warm breeze with optional views of the beach. Considering that, what follows are guidelines for a casual concert in warmer weather.

From your capsule wardrobe: Make sure that you have your sunscreen, even if the day is overcast. This is arguably the most important thing you'll put on for this event. Also grab your sunglasses.

In your **20s**: Add linen shorts with a tank top and gladiator sandals.

In your **30s**: Add a linen skirt with a tank top and thong sandals.

In your **40s**: Add a maxi dress with a sun hat and flat sandals.

In your **50s**: Add a small crossbody bag with a shirt dress and flat sandals.

If you're a **triangle** body type: Consider both cut and color when looking for tops that have interesting or lightly embellished necklines or cut-outs and/or are in bold colors.

If you're an **inverted triangle** body type: Consider hues like olive, mustard and navy, and make sure they're concentrated near the lower half of your body.

If you're a **rectangle** body type: Look for pieces that emphasize and accentuate your waistline.

If you're a **diamond** body type: Concentrate lighter colors like blush and camel toward the top half of your body.

If you're an **apple** body type: Look for slightly lower necklines and avoid anything too fitted.

If you're an **hourglass** body type: Consider a print on your top and coordinating colors throughout the rest of your look.

Barbecue

Whether they're held in your best friend's backyard or in a sprawling park, barbecues are a great chance to get together with friends and family. They're also a great chance to showcase a much more casual style.

From your capsule wardrobe: Just like an outdoor concert, barbecues demand that you have both your sunscreen and sunglasses on hand and that you use them both.

In your **20s**: Add a print dress, a denim jacket and wedge sandals. If you're petite make sure the print is small, if you're plus-size select a larger scale print.

In your **30s**: Add a tank top and a colorblocked or printed maxi skirt with flat sandals and a straw tote bag.

In your **40s**: Add printed pants, a tee shirt and ballerina flats or flat sandals.

In your **50s**: Add linen drawstring pants and a blouse with ballerina flats or flat sandals.

If you're a **triangle** body type: Consider layering a series of necklaces of different lengths to create some interest near the neckline, and concentrate any darker colors in your outfit toward the bottom of your look.

If you're an **inverted triangle** body type: Look for clothing options where the main area of interest is on the bottom. This includes selecting boldly colored footwear or looking for patterns that are more concentrated on the lower half.

If you're a **rectangle** body type: Find an interesting way to incorporate a belt or sash into your look. Consider that even without belt loops, this can be done.

If you're a **diamond** body type: Focus on darker hues that are still bright, such as a candy apple red and avoid prints on your top.

If you're an **apple** body type: Consider hi-lo tops which don't hug your midriff and add some interest to a look with minimal effort.

If you're an **hourglass** body type: Consider variations of a print in an all over look e.g. if you're wearing printed pants then add flats with a similar print, and consider a top that utilizes one of the secondary colors in the pattern for a look that pops but isn't overly matched.

Girl's Night Out

Maybe your going to a great new lounge for martinis or going to check out a movie, no matter what the reason you're heading out is, it's important that you look amazing.

From your capsule wardrobe: Your black or nude pumps. The importance of comfortable footwear cannot be understated. Also, grab your oversized clutch so that you can easily carry all of your essentials.

In your **20s**: Add a mini-skirt with a silk tank and a statement necklace.

In your **30s**: Add skinny jeans and a sequined tank and bracelets.

In your **40s**: Add leather or waxed denim pants with a blazer and a silk top.

In your **50s**: Add your emergency dress. If it's black, also add a pop of color with a boldly colored pashima wrap and a cocktail ring.

If you're a **triangle** body type: Look for a top with an interesting neckline or layer for an interesting look e.g. a longer lace tank under your tank or blouse can create interest, texture or show a great peek of a different fabric.

If you're an **inverted triangle** body type: Consider darker colors such as navy, chocolate or charcoal gray for your bottom.

If you're a **rectangle** body type: Select pieces with a similar fit on both the top and the bottom e.g. if your top is form-fitting also opt for a form-fitting bottom.

If you're a **diamond** body type: Look for a top with minimal texture near your stomach e.g. if you're wearing a sequined tank look for one with a spray of sequins near the bust line as opposed to all over. Also, ensure that your top is not too tight.

If you're an **apple** body type: Consider a bold colored bottom with a neutral colored top e.g. you may opt for a teal bottom with a black top.

If you're an **hourglass** body type: Watch your proportions carefully e.g. if you're wearing a miniskirt, the natural instinct may be to also opt for a tank with a more revealing neckline but select something more demure.

An evening in

Perhaps it's your first night alone with your partner or a special anniversary or maybe it's just a random Tuesday. Whatever the reason, there are times that your style isn't about what you're wearing out but what you're sharing with someone special in your life.

From your capsule wardrobe: You may want to add a pair of pearls or your cocktail ring, but neither piece is really necessary in this instance and it's addition or omission will completely be a matter of personal preference.

In your **20s**: Channel a vintage vibe with a retro-inspired corset complete with garters and make it more your own with the addition of patterned or lace thigh-highs and bright stilettos.

In your **30s**: Try something unexpected like a tie-front bra and side tie panties.

In your **40s**: Opt for a sleek kimono in a dark hue and pair it with a pair of brightly colored heels for an unexpected pop of color.

In your **50s**: Feel flirty and feminine in a short nightgown in a rich color like black or blood red. Pick a fabric like silk or a lush satin, and pair it with your Louboutins.

If you're a **triangle** body type: Consider something with a lace trim or lace overlay on the bust line and opt for a brighter/bolder bottom.

If you're an **inverted triangle** body type: Look for tops with demi-cups and/or with a pattern and coordinate your bottom.

If you're a **rectangle** body type: Don't attempt to cinch your waist at all and instead select pieces that fit you well and work with your body type as opposed to trying to alter it.

If you're a **diamond** body type: Consider a bold all over color like cerulean blue and play up what you feel are your best assets.

If you're an **apple** body type: Don't shy away from something that shows off your midsection. As long as the piece makes you feel amazing that's what matters most.

If you're an **hourglass** body type: Now's the time to work your curves to their full potential. Consider pretty patterns, interesting textures and anything else that catches your fancy.

This chapter offers just a small taste of what a stylist can do for you, taking the guess work out of what to wear while ensuring that you look amazing and can showcase your personality.

Chapter 9: Who. What. Wear. Pt. 2

"Girls do not dress for boys. They dress for themselves and of course each other. If girls dressed for boys they'd just walk around naked at all times." -Betsey Johnson

As difficult as it may be to select "the outfit" for events like job interviews or concerts, it can be even more daunting to find the piece you're looking for when something like a wedding or fashion week rolls around. And, of course, this process is multiplied when you need to pack for multi-day events. While a stylist will be your best friend in situations like these, here's a bit of a primer so that you're never in a situation where you don't have some basic answer to the question of what to wear.

Reunions

Whether it's been 10 years or three times as long, reunions offer a chance to see old friends and of course show off how fabulous you are.

High School

Especially when you're in your twenties, high school reunions serve as an important chance to showcase how you've grown and how gracefully you've done it.

From your capsule wardrobe: Your emergency dress. This is already a piece that you feel comfortable and chic in, and so you'll be able to wear it with complete confidence.

In your **20s**: Add a pair of pumps and a jeweled or oversized clutch.

In your **30s**: Add a pair of boldly colored pumps and a coordinating clutch

In your **40s**: Add a belt to your dress and top the look off with a boyfriend blazer and pumps.

In your **50s**: Add a wrap sweater and your Louboutin pumps.

If you're a **triangle** body type: Consider adding some structure to your shoulders with removable shoulder pads in your emergency dress. A little height goes a long way in creating a more striking proportion.

If you're an **inverted triangle** body type: Look for a lace underskirt to add under your dress, provided it has a fuller skirt. In the event that your dress has a straight skirt, consider the addition of patterned pumps or stilettos to draw the eye downward.

If you're a **rectangle** body type: Add a boldly colored or printed obi belt to your dress for a more proportional look. If you select a pattern, remember that if you're petite the pattern should be delicate and if you're plus size the pattern should be more dramatic. Consider that, while leather obi belts are super stylish, those made from a softer fabric are more flexible and provide you with more styling options.

If you're a **diamond** body type: Add a wide belt or sash in a dark hue to your emergency dress, creating a flattering break in your silhouette.

If you're an **apple** body type: Consider your accessories carefully, focusing on incorporating a statement necklace or earrings which will draw the eye upward.

If you're an **hourglass** body type: Accentuate your curves by adding a thin belt in a bold color or pattern to your emergency dress.

College

Whether you're looking to catch up with sorority sisters that you haven't had a chance to see in years or just looking forward to a chance to show off how much or how little you've changed, college reunions offer the perfect chance to do both.

From your capsule wardrobe: Following the formula of the high school reunion select your emergency dress for this event. It's an effortless piece that should always make you feel at ease and elegant when you wear it which makes it especially amazing to be the centerpiece of an outfit.

In your **30s**: Add a colorful kimono that matches the length of your dress along with your Louboutin or nude pumps based on the colors of your other pieces and a clutch.

In your **40s**: Add a patterned pump and a coordinating clutch.

In your **50s**: Add sheer nude or black hose, your Louboutin pumps and a black evening bag.

If you're a **triangle** body type: Layer on the necklaces or find a single statement necklace to keep the eyes drawn upward.

If you're an **inverted triangle** body type: Opt for a fringe overskirt in the same color as your dress for an unexpected accent.

If you're a **rectangle** body type: Add a thin jeweled belt to draw attention to your waistline.

If you're a **diamond** body type: Add a wide sash in the same color as your emergency dress utilizing a different fabric.

If you're an **apple** body type: Adding something like a brightly colored blazer or wrap draw attention to that piece while still letting your overall look shine.

If you're an **hourglass** body type: Consider adding texture to your look with a faux or real alligator or pony skin belt in a bright color, such as coral or yellow or a wide sash in silk or satin.

Weddings

Unless you're a bridesmaid, prepping for someone else's nuptials isn't simply about getting the right gift and getting to the ceremony on time, it's also about making sure that you're not overdressed or under dressed for their big day.

Casual

Casual weddings are laid back affairs where the guests aren't very dressed up.

From your capsule wardrobe: Black or nude pumps and your oversized clutch. These pieces are the building blocks that the rest of your look will be built around.

In your **20s**: Add a cocktail-length or knee length dress. It can have a print on it but make sure that it suits you, which is an especially important point to keep in mind if you're plus size and/or petite. Also note that it shouldn't have any jeweled or sparkly embellishments, like Swarovski crystals or sequins.

In your **30s**: Add a knee-length or calf-length A-line dress or sheath dress. Avoid fabrics that are too formal and instead, depending on season and venue, select a cotton blend or something with leather or suede.

In your **40s**: Add a silk shirt dress. Where this is a casual style, the silk element makes it appropriate for a wedding

In your **50s**: add a cap sleeve sheath dress in a bold color with your basic pumps

If you're a **triangle** body type: Add an intriguing necklace that doesn't have any jewels e.g. something with a large hammered gold pendant or select a dress with an interesting neckline.

If you're an **inverted triangle** body type: Look for a dress where the skirt has some flare or select an ombre piece where the color is concentrated from the waist downward.

If you're a **rectangle** body type: Look for a dress that will allow you to add a belt which will aid in you looking more evenly proportioned.

If you're a **diamond** body type: Stay away from anything with an empire or otherwise high waistline and look for more classically shaped dresses such as an a-line.

If you're an **apple** body type: Look for a dress that isn't tight around your midsection but is still form fitting.

If you're an **hourglass** body type: Select an area of your body that you want to highlight. If you opt for a higher hemline to show off your legs then look for a dress that has longer sleeves.

Semi-formal

Semi-formal weddings are a bit like cocktail parties, there's a bit of glitz and guests are more dressed up.

From your capsule wardrobe: Your Chanel pearls or cocktail ring, something to ensure that you have a bit of sparkle.

In your **20s**: Add a plain cocktail dress and a pair of coordinating stilettos or jeweled sandals along with a clutch.

In your **30s**: Add a cocktail dress with or without some minor embellishments, a pair of pumps and a clutch.

In your **40s**: Add a sheath or cocktail dress, a pair of pumps and a clutch.

In your **50s**: Add your crisp white button up embellished with a brooch, a knee-length a-line skirt and a pair of heels. Complete the look with a clutch.

If you're a **triangle** body type: Make sure that you're wearing something with an interesting neckline and/or that the embellishments are at the top of your dress/shirt to ensure that's where the focus is.

If you're an **inverted triangle** body type: Try to find an interesting shoe or a dress that has detailing from the waist downward.

If you're a **rectangle** body type: Either seek out a dress with built-in corseting or one with a more overall structured shape.

If you're a **diamond** body type: Look for a dress or skirt with a drop waist to help elongate your torso and create better proportions.

If you're an **apple** body type: Focus on a piece that flatters your assets, this may include one with a low neckline, simple detailing on the back or one that shows off your arms or legs.

If you're an **hourglass** body type: Avoid any piece that's too loosely or too tightly structured. You don't want anything that hides your body. you want something that shows your curves without overtly showing them off.

Beach Formal

Whether it's a grand destination wedding on a pink sand beach in the Bahamas or a more intimate affair on a local beach closer to home, beach weddings are a popular option and it makes sense to be as prepared as possible.

From your capsule wardrobe: Sunglasses and sunscreen. Even overcast days can be dangerous in terms of UV rays so make sure that you pack these two essentials.

In your **20s**: Add a cocktail length dress and flat metallic colored sandals along with a clutch. Colors like coral, mint and lavender look lovely on a variety of skin tones and pair well with silver, gold or rose-gold colored sandals.

In your **30s**: Add a cocktail, knee-length or maxi dress and metallic or jeweled sandals with a clutch.

In your **40s**: Add a short caftan or cocktail dress, jeweled sandals and a clutch.

In your **50s**: Add a short caftan or knee-length dress and metallic or jeweled sandals.

If you're a **triangle** body type: Look for a dress with an embellished neckline or low cut. Additionally, if you're going with a print, find one that's bolder at the top.

If you're an **inverted triangle** body type: Try a dress in a subtle ombre that goes from light to dark or with a pattern that has a similar gradation.

If you're a **rectangle** body type: Look for something that has ruching or an embellishment near the waist. If you're wearing a caftan that isn't naturally cinched at the waist, a sash or an obi belt makes a great addition.

If you're a **diamond** body type: Look for either an empire or drop waist or something with a low neckline to create the most flattering look.

If you're an **apple** body type: Avoid anything that's too tight around your midsection and select a fabric that has a bit of stretch.

If you're an **hourglass** body type: If you're selecting a dress with embellishments or a pattern, make sure that it's balanced so you maintain your proportions.

Formal

Also referred to as "black-tie optional" this is a wedding where darker tones and sleeker attire is expected but you can still showcase a style all your own.

From your capsule wardrobe: Chanel Pearls or cocktail ring. These are the perfect accents to an outfit that is meant to be dressed up.

In your **20s**: Add a cocktail dress in a silk or satin, opting for rich jewel tones such as emerald green, sapphire blue and ruby red which look good on a variety of skin tones. Pair it with a pair of jeweled stiletto or Louboutin peep-toes or pumps, and a coordinating clutch.

In your **30s**: Add a cocktail, knee-length or calf-length sheath dress in colors like wine, slate gray or navy. Pair it with a jeweled clutch and pumps or peep-toes.

In your **40s**: Add a knee-length or calf-length dress in colors like eggplant, hunter green or dark gray. Pair it with metallic pumps or peep-toes in rose gold or platinum and a clutch.

In your **50s**: Opt for either a silk skirt suit in shades like ox blood or citrine which are powerful and unexpected. Pair it with a coordinating fascinator, pumps and a clutch.

If you're a **triangle** body type: Find a dress or suit jacket with embellishments near the neckline or at the bust.

If you're an **inverted triangle** body type: Look for dresses or suit jackets that offer more embellishment near the waist, a peplum, flare or over skirt to provide options to help you look more proportioned.

If you're a **rectangle** body type: Beading, ruching or other embellishments near the waist help to draw the eye there for a more flattering look.

If you're a **diamond** body type: Avoid fabrics that are too tight around your midsection and look for something with embellishments at both the top and bottom for a more proportional look.

If you're an **apple** body type: Opt for something with a lower neckline that is still appropriate, also a little beading on the hemline is also helpful.

If you're an **hourglass** body type: Opt for something plain or with an all-over embellishment for a look that's the most flattering.

Black-tie

Both chic cocktail dresses and evening gowns are appropriate for this type of wedding where glamor and elegance are a must.

From your capsule wardrobe: Add your oversized clutch and build a look of coordinating colors around it.

In your **20s**: Add an embellished cocktail dress and coordinating stilettos in either a metallic or jewel tone.

In your **30s**: Add an evening gown with an unexpected element such as a high neckline or a plunging back, along with heels in a coordinating color.

In your **40s**: Add silk palazzo pants in a dark hue, a corset top with or without embellishments and a silk wrap. Pair it with stiletto heels or jeweled sandals.

In your **50s**: Add an evening gown and a statement necklace or chandelier earrings. Finish the look with pumps or kitten heels.

If you're a **triangle** body type: Then the focal point of your look should be above your waist. This can be achieved on the look itself with beading or a bold color or it can be added with accessories such as an eye-catching necklace.

If you're an **inverted triangle** body type: Then you'll want the wow-factor of your look to be on your bottom half. This can include beading that is along the hemline of your dress, a high slit or palazzo pants that mimic tuxedo pants with the signature stripe on the legs.

If you're a **rectangle** body type: Opt for a look where your midsection is the focal point. This can be achieved with a jeweled belt or bridal sash (just make sure the bride isn't wearing one that's similar) or can be a part of your dress.

If you're a **diamond** body type: Avoid any fabrics that will be too stiff and keep any intricate or large detail work away from your midsection.

If you're an **apple** body type: Opt for darker hues and try to put together a look where there are similar details near both the neckline and hemline. This can be achieved in part by selecting something with a jeweled or detailed hemline and adding a necklace with a similar feel.

If you're an **hourglass** body type: Feel free to select a color that's a bit bolder such as a lush coral tone and allowing it to be the focal point of your look.

White-tie

These functions are the very height of high society formality and, as such, offer the perfect opportunity for ball gowns and especially elegant accessories.

From your capsule wardrobe: Add your Chanel pearls or cocktail ring. Similar to a formal affair for a white-tie event you want accents that complement a dressed-up look.

In your **20s**: Add a sequin gown with a stiletto heel and an evening bag. To avoid it looking like a prom look, select a gown in a shade such as black or gray and avoid anything with an ombre effect.

In your **30s**: Add a gown that has beautiful beadwork in an unexpected but flattering color. For example, if you have very fair skin you may want to opt for an almost black shade of blue while if you have a darker skin tone you may want to select something in an oxblood, aubergine or peach. Finish your look with coordinating heels and a beaded clutch.

In your **40s**: Select a sleek and well-fitting gown and pair it with opera length gloves and a clutch.

In your **50s**: Be daring in separates with a mix of amazing textures by selecting a floor length skirt that's beaded or has a lace overlay, paired with a silk or chiffon top, a fur shawl (faux or real), satin clutch and coordinating heels. To keep the look cohesive keep everything in the same color family. For example, if you're utilizing white or gray fur for your shawl then both lavender and red would look amazing as the main color for the rest of your look.

If you're a **triangle** body type: Keep the focus of your look near your neckline. Keep in mind that this can also be done by having a look with interesting shoulder details.

If you're an **inverted triangle** body type: Avoid anything where the top of the look is especially detailed or intricate and instead draw the eye downward.

If you're a **rectangle** body type: Don't be afraid of a bit of flare near your waist, peplums are a good way of achieving this.

If you're a **diamond** body type: Look for fabrics that have either flow or stretch, but avoid anything with a tent like appearance.

If you're an **apple** body type: Look for a hemline that has extra detail that includes beading or jewels and isn't too heavy.

If you're an **hourglass** body type: Feel free to go for an overall overlay, such as lace or look for something that is beaded all over.

Extra special occurrences

Movie premieres, interviews and book signings certainly aren't the type of thing that most people do everyday, but they could be in your future someday. While you can always, and certainly should, call a stylist when and if it happens, here's a bit of insight into how to dress for extra-special occasions.

Red carpet event

Whether you're attending on the arm of someone, flying solo or there on a date, it's likely that there'll be paparazzi somewhere at one of these events and just in case your image is snapped you want to be sure that you look smashing. Keep in mind that if you're personally a part of the project as one of the actresses that it may be important that you convey a certain image, and in that regard a consultation with the team is in order before you contact a stylist for their input. In any other situation, the following looks are interesting without being over the top and will have people talking in a good way.

From your capsule wardrobe: Select your Louboutin pumps along with your cocktail ring for great starter pieces to an overall look that will be all about getting people to look in your direction and comment on how stylish you are.

In your **20s**: Add a patterned mini-dress and a small satin clutch in a color that coordinates well.

In your **30s**: Add leather or leather-look skinnies, a sheer sleeveless blouse along with a jeweled clutch.

In your **40s**: Add tuxedo pants and a silk tank top with a minaudiere.

In your **50s**: Add your white button-up with a knee-length satin wrap-skirt and a clutch.

If you're a **triangle** body type: Look for a well-fitting top that contours to your body. When wearing a dress, select something where the neckline is interesting and/or embellished.

If you're an **inverted triangle** body type: Select darker colors to wear up top. Note that black isn't your only option and that a rich shade or green, purple or blue would look amazing on any skin tone.

If you're a **rectangle** body type: Add interest near your waistline. In a dress, this can be done with color blocking or a thin jeweled belt. A thin jeweled belt would also look amazing with skinnies or tuxedo pants. For a wrap-skirt, add a brooch off center along the waistline.

If you're a **diamond** body type: Add a fitted blazer that matches the color of your top or the top half of your dress.

If you're an **apple** body type: Look for fabrics that have stretch, such as jersey, and seek out pieces that are well fitting and not tent like.

If you're an **hourglass** body type: Consider more structured fabrics, such as leather, to truly highlight your figure.

Front row at fashion week

The front row at fashion week isn't simply a prime place to see the latest collections grace the catwalk, it's also a prime place to be seen and you want to be sure that no one has anything to say other than that you were dressed exquisitely. Beyond that, the goal is to be the picture of understated elegance and bonus points if what you're wearing is something from the line of the designer whose show you're going to be watching.

From your capsule wardrobe: Your Louboutin pumps. They're eternally in style without being too trendy.

In your **20s**: Add skinny jeans or leather or leather-look skinnies, a sleeveless blouse and a blazer.

In your **30s**: Add a leather pencil skirt and a silk tank top.

In your **40s**: Add wool/jersey or wool/silk skinny pants and a silk blouse.

In your **50s**: Add a silk crepe blazer, a blouse and cigarette pants.

If you're a **triangle** body type: Opt for blazers that are sleeveless or blouses that are textured.

If you're an **inverted triangle** body type: Select a bottom that is a dark hue. Black is a classic choice but you may also want to select a shade like gray or a deep pink color, both of which look good on all skin tones.

If you're a **rectangle** body type: Emphasize the lines of your body with pieces that are form-fitting, and forgo a belt that will draw too much attention to your waist.

If you're a **diamond** body type: If you're wearing a blazer make sure that it's the same color as your blouse and opt for both in a darker hue. If you're not wearing a blazer just keep your top dark.

If you're an **apple** body type: Opt for the most classic cut you can find for your bottom and experiment when it comes to the neckline of your top.

If you're an **hourglass** body type: Feel free to add a print to your look, just keep proportions in mind which means something small scale if you're petite and something bolder if you're plus-size.

A political gala

Whether you or your significant other is running for office or you're there in support of the candidate, you want to be sure that your look is both polished and politically correct.

From your capsule wardrobe: Your Chanel pearls are perfect for this occasion which requires formal wear and classic fashion choices.

In your **20s**: Add a floor length evening gown with nude or black pumps and a clutch.

In your **30s**: Add a tulle or doupioni ball-skirt and a long-sleeved silk blouse with coordinating pumps and a clutch.

In your **40s**: Add a tea-length gown in silk or chiffon with Louboutin pumps and an evening bag.

In your **50s**: Add a formal skirt suit and coordinating pumps with a clutch.

If you're a **triangle** body type: Opt for an off the shoulder as opposed to completely sleeveless look, or select a top with an interesting yet still modest neckline.

If you're an **inverted triangle** body type: Avoid shoulder pads or a high neckline and opt for a flared skirt or a dress with a flared bottom.

If you're a **rectangle** body type: Don't worry about accentuating your waist as much as finding pieces that are flattering to your natural shape.

If you're a **diamond** body type: Opt for darker hues near the top of your look.

If you're an **apple** body type: Select darker hues for the entirety of your outfit.

If you're an **hourglass** body type: Avoid any piece that isn't demure. You don't need to opt for a look that's matronly or funeral, but select pieces that are decidedly modest.

For a television appearance

There are numerous reasons you could end up on television, perhaps you're promoting a new book or product, or speaking out about an issue that's important to you. Or maybe you've landed a role on a reality show. Whatever the reason you want to make sure that you and your clothes are ready for your close up. Note that in the case of the latter, there may be very specific requirements regarding wardrobe e.g. you may be expected to be in a certain color or a style that typifies a certain character, so before consulting a stylist, consult whoever has booked the appearance. You'll also want to do something similar in the event that you're appearing on a religious or political program as there may be certain guidelines that you need to adhere to.

From your capsule wardrobe: Your emergency dress. This is a piece that you're already comfortable in and you know that there'll be no wardrobe malfunction if you have it on.

In your **20s**: Add a statement necklace and a pair of coordinating stilettos.

In your **30s**: Add a pair of earrings and a bracelet along with your Louboutins.

In your **40s**: Add a boldly colored blazer and your Louboutins.

In your **50s**: Add your Chanel pearls and a pair of pumps

If you're a **triangle** body type: To balance out your proportions, ensure that your heels are black or nude, and not attention grabbing.

If you're an **inverted triangle** body type: Avoid necklaces or large earrings and stick to pieces like bracelets and cocktail rings.

If you're a **rectangle** body type: Add a slim belt or sash to your waist in a coordinating color to your dress.

If you're a **diamond** body type: Add a wide sash in the same color as your dress.

If you're an **apple** body type: Make sure that your accessories are bold, but not garish, so that they perfectly complement your look.

If you're an **hourglass** body type: Note that, if you'd like, you can add a patterned blazer or bold heels for a more personalized look without skewing your proportions.

For a personal appearance

Being involved in a key way with a charity, acting as a spokesperson or being linked to a political candidate are just a few reasons why you'd be required to make a personal appearance. Make sure that the impression you make is a fashionable one.

From your capsule wardrobe: Your white button-up shirt and black or nude pumps are key pieces that are also low key, which helps to keep you looking polished without stealing the spotlight from the issue that you're supporting.

In your **20s**: Swap out your white button-up for your white t-shirt and add a blazer along with skinny trousers and a statement accessory.

In your **30s**: Add a patterned pencil-skirt and swap out your black or nude pumps for your Louboutins.

In your **40s**: Add a pair of well-fitting trousers and a statement accessory based on your body type.

In your **50s**: Add a knee-length silk skirt and your Chanel pearls along with a Pashima wrap

If you're a **triangle** body type: Make your statement accessory a great necklace or pair of earrings, or if you're wearing a blazer or wrap opt for one in an interesting color or pattern. If you're wearing pencil-skirt opt for one on a solid hue as opposed to one with a pattern.

If you're an **inverted triangle** body type: Make your statement accessory something like a beautiful cuff bracelet or cocktail ring, or if you're wearing a blazer or wrap opt for a white one. For your pencil-skirt, select a pattern based on your proportions e.g. if you're petite select a delicate pattern and if you're plus-size opt for a bolder pattern.

If you're a **rectangle** body type: To show off your shape, look for pieces that are slightly boxier and with a skirt nix your button-up for a blouse that will allow for a fuller, less stiff look.

If you're a **diamond** body type: If you're wearing a blazer or a wrap opt for a white one, one with a tone-on-tone pattern can be particularly striking. In pants, add a medium to wide belt and if wearing a pencil-skirt opt for color blocking or one where the waistband is clearly defined as separate from the rest of the skirt.

If you're an **apple** body type: Opt for trousers or a skirt in a bold color, such as turquoise or ruby, and focus on finding accessories that accentuate the look.

If you're an **hourglass** body type: Don't overdress your look by adding too many accessories, instead focus on accentuating the lines of your body.

<u>**Multi-day events**</u>

Packing for a multi-day event can be difficult, but it doesn't have to be. Whether it's a few days with your best girlfriends, a business trip or anything in between it's best that you have some idea about the basics of what you'll need.

Weekend with your best friends

A weekend with your best friends will mean different things for different people. For some, it'll be a weekend with just the girls while for others it'll be a trip for couples or old friends of both sexes from high school and/or college. Whatever the configuration of travelers, you want to be sure that you have everything that you need to ensure that you look great for any situation that may arise. Keep in mind that these suggestions are based on a casual trip and include pieces that'll work in any weather. If your trip has a specific purpose or will be taking you somewhere where you need to be particularly aware of the climate, then consult whoever is planning the trip and then consult a stylist directly for more precise directions.

From your capsule wardrobe: Cashmere duster or cardigan, emergency dress, ballet flats, black or nude pumps, jeans, white tee, handbag, oversized clutch and sunscreen. Over the course of two or three days and one or two nights, you truly shouldn't need much more than this.

In your **20s**: Add a bathing suit, a pair of flat sneakers and a mini skirt.

In your **30s**: Add a cocktail dress, a pair of flat sneakers, a sequin and silk or satin tank top.

In your **40s**: Add a blazer, a pencil-skirt and some canvas slip-ons.

In your **50s**: Add a caftan, crepe jersey cigarette pants and a Pashmina wrap.

If you're a **triangle** body type: Pack statement necklaces and earrings, and look for tops with interesting or embellished necklines or tops that are boldly colored while keeping your bottom pieces in more muted hues and tones.

If you're an **inverted triangle** body type: Pack bottoms in bold colors or those with embellished hems. Also, look for brightly colored or patterned shoes to help draw the eye downward.

If you're a **rectangle** body type: Pack boxier pieces to show off your shape or a mix of belts and sashes for greater proportions.

If you're a **diamond** body type: Pack wide belts in solid colors along with statement necklaces.

If you're an **apple** body type: Pack pieces that are form-fitting and not tight, and focus on the addition of statement necklaces and earrings.

If you're an **hourglass** body type: Pack pieces in classic cuts that are interesting in terms of color or pattern.

Weekend with your significant other

Whether it's your first weekend away together or a trip that you've been taking every year for the past decade, a weekend trip with your partner is a great chance to reconnect with each other and the last thing you should have to worry about is what you're going to wear. The suggestions below are for a more casual trip and will work in a variety of weather conditions. Keep in mind that if you know you're traveling to a location that's especially warm or cold that tweaks will need to be made. Additionally, the purpose of your trip may dictate what extra pieces you pack so be sure to talk to your significant other and then consult a stylist for the best wardrobe choices.

From your capsule wardrobe: Your emergency dress, ballet flats, black or nude pumps, jeans, white tee, handbag, oversized clutch, red lipstick and sunscreen. These are arguably the most classic of all of your pieces and, as such, they pair especially well with each other and with anything else you'll pack. In addition to these pieces also consult Chapter 8 for what to wear for "an evening in" and add that to your bag as well if you're planning on being intimate.

In your **20s**: Add flat sneakers, a denim jacket and mini dress.

In your **30s**: Add a bandage skirt, a silk blouse and a leather or leather-look jacket.

In your **40s**: Add a maxi dress, a pencil-skirt and a sheer blouse.

In your **50s**: Add your cashmere duster, a short-sleeved blouse and a knee-length skirt.

If you're a **triangle** body type: Pack tops with patterns, keeping in mind to keep the designs small if you're petite and bolder if you're plus-size. Also add statement earrings.

If you're an **inverted triangle** body type: Pack bottoms in bold colors or those that are textured or in interesting fabrics.

If you're a **rectangle** body type: Pack pieces with a slightly sportier flair, these can be sporty pieces in feminine colors or with feminine details, or more standard pieces in darker hues or with details such as mesh. You don't want anything that looks like a costume, just clothing that acts as a complement to your more athletic frame.

If you're a **diamond** body type: Pack pieces with distinct waistbands or add a few wide belts to your bag in a variety of colors.

If you're an **apple** body type: Pack a variety of colors and opt for top pieces with minimal texture. Opt for bottoms that are well-fitted and skirts with higher hemlines.

If you're an **hourglass** body type: Pack pieces that are boldly colored and opt for patterns when possible. Textured pieces are alright as long as they don't add bulk.

Business trip

On a business trip, no matter where you're going you want your wardrobe to be fairly conservative. While this may differ based on your exact field, this is the rule in the corporate world. For this reason, while pops of color and pretty patterns are okay, you want to avoid pieces that are too revealing.

From your capsule wardrobe: Your blazer, white button-down shirt, Louboutins, classic handbag, emergency dress and Chanel pearls are all pieces that will serve you well.

In your **20s**: Add your ballet flats, a silk tank and silk jersey cigarette pants.

In your **30s**: Add a silk blouse, wool jersey skinny pants and a knee-length silk wrap skirt.

In your **40s**: Add a sleeveless blouse, a knee-length pencil skirt and a shirt dress.

In your **50s**: Add your cashmere cardigan or duster, a wrap dress and skinny leg trousers.

If you're a **triangle** body type: Pack delicate necklaces and small earrings to help frame your face and accent your top. Also, opt for tops in powerful hues like navy, red and hunter green.

If you're an **inverted triangle** body type: Pack bottoms that are perfectly tailored and in darker hues such as gray and black.

If you're a **rectangle** body type: Pack thin belts in subtle patterns or colors that pop.

If you're a **diamond** body type: Pack pieces in complimentary tones, making sure that in every outfit one color family is on top and another is on the bottom.

If you're an **apple** body type: Pack pieces that are well-fitting and select more lightweight materials for a fit that is flattering without being bulky.

If you're an **hourglass** body type: Pack pieces that have interesting details that aren't overpowering, such as a thin pinstripe or herringbone pattern.

Allow each of these outfits to serve you as a guideline and then look for alternative possibilities. With the assistance of a great stylist, you can inject your own personality into these pairings for a look that's more personal and even more stylish.

Chapter 10: Pampering Yourself

"I believe in manicures. I believe in overdressing. I believe in primping at leisure and wearing lipstick..." - Audrey Hepburn

Life is full of little luxuries, indulgences that make us feel better and, in turn, make us look better. By pampering yourself, you can elevate your personal style from good to great and elevate everything you wear into a look that truly sparkles.

Skin

Proper skincare is essential and encompasses everything from the way you wash your face in the morning to what types of spa treatments you choose. This doesn't mean that you need to spend hundreds or even thousands of dollars on expensive face and body creams, but it does mean that you need to learn what type of skin you have and the best ways to care for it. Finding and working closely with a licensed esthetician can aid you in finding a routine that it best suited for you as an individual. Additionally, be sure to contact a reputable dermatologist before tackling any issues such as eczema or hormonal acne. These things are completely manageable, but you want to make sure that you're getting the best possible insight and information available.

Regardless of skin type, though, there are some general tips that everyone can benefit from.

First, always remove your make-up. After a long day at work or a long night out you may not always want to remove your make-up, but we all know that leaving it on is not the best thing for your skin and depending on the products you're using they can also stain your linens. So take the few minutes necessary to take it all off.

Secondly, be sure to utilize sunscreen. Keep in mind that this is necessary even on overcast days or in the winter if you'll be outdoors for an extended period of time.

Next, be aware of when you're scheduling spa treatments or tanning sessions. Certain procedures can leave your skin extra sensitive and so going out immediately following something like a facial is likely not the best idea.

Finally, always exercise caution before undergoing any cosmetic procedures. Even routine things that can be done within the office of a doctor, with little or no anesthesia, can be detrimental to you in the long run if the person performing them isn't properly trained. Recommendations can be a big help in this area but you'll also want to do your own research to make sure that your standards are met. A good place to start is by finding out whether or not the plastic surgeon you're planning on working with is board certified by the American Society of Plastic Surgeons.

After ensuring that your basic skincare needs are met, be sure to reward yourself. There are numerous ways this can be done. Try indulging in a full body massage to help you relax or try out some new make-up colors or techniques which are key in helping to create a complete overall look.

Hair

Whether you have tresses that go well past your shoulders or prefer something much shorter, having healthy hair should be a priority. If you don't already have a hairstylist that you go to exclusively, be sure to audition a few. This should include getting a feel for what types of hair types they work best on, talking to past clients if possible and going to them on several trips with different needs. While you may be tempted to immediately try something exciting like a shorter cut or a bolder color, start with baby steps like a trim or a few highlights, which will give you a way to develop a rapport without making any major changes.

Keep in mind that working closely with a professional hairstylist will help you get the lushest locks possible, but there are some things that every woman can and should do on her own.

Make sure that you're being good to your hair and aren't overwhelming it with products or potentially damaging treatments. Learn your hair type and pay attention to what it can and can't handle, and what you should be doing to maintain a beautiful mane. Also, keep in mind that similar to the way in which prolonged sun exposure can damage your skin that it can have similar effects on your hair, and so for a day at the beach you may want to wrap it up in a chic scarf or turban that complements your bathing suit.

Take the time to learn about and understand your face shape. Your face shape plays a large role in determining what types of hair cuts will also be most flattering. Similarly, be sure to keep your skin tone in mind as well, as it should play a factor in what color or colors will look best in your hair.

Don't discount wigs, weaves or extensions. When you're contemplating a color change, a drastic new style, growing out or cutting your hair, a well made wig, an expert weave or some well placed extensions can help you decide if the look is right for you. While there are some amazing programs that allow for digital make-overs, if you can, make the time to try these things out in person as they'll let you feel as well as see the look. Wigs, weaves and extensions are also great if you're looking for a temporary change or like the idea of a lot of different options for your hair without having to worry about whether or not you're damaging your hair.

Remember that the hair on your head isn't the only hair on your body that deserves your attention. Good grooming means also taking care of your eyebrow, underarm and leg hair, as well as the hair in your bikini area. Be mindful of any waxes or hair removal products that you're using, or if you're having them removed by a professional make sure that you both get recommendations and do your own individual research.

Nails

Some women love the chic look of a classic French manicure while others prefer bolder colors. Making time for a mani-pedi is a small thing that can have a huge impact on both how well you look and feel. Find a manicurist that's sanitary, who creates the styles that complement you and your wardrobe, and treasure him or her.

A good stylist will help you dress better, a great stylist will encourage you to feel better. And feeling better is about being able to be comfortable in your skin, knowing that you're well cared for from head to toe.

Chapter 11: Styling For Men

"Clothes and manners do not make the man; but when he is made, they greatly improve his appearance."- Arthur Ashe

What lingerie is for men is what a well-tailored suit is for women. There's something instantly attractive about a gentleman who is well dressed, something that everyone responds to, even if only briefly. Being well dressed is essentially about three key things: understanding your body shape, building a versatile wardrobe and being well-groomed.

Body Shapes

Before anyone goes shopping for themselves or for someone else, it's ideal that the body shape of the person who will be wearing the clothes is known. For men there are five basic body shapes. The body shapes are the triangle, the inverted triangle, the rectangle, the oval, and the trapezoid.

Men with a **triangle** body shape are larger on the bottom half of their bodies than they are on the top half, and their chests are narrower than their hips. Jackets with shoulder pads help to create a more balanced silhouette as do shirts with narrower seams.

Men who have an **inverted triangle** body shape have broad shoulders and chests with narrower waists and legs. Well-fitting and tailored shirts help to accentuate a strongly sculpted upper body and paired with straight leg well tailored pants a balanced silhouette is created.

Men who have the **rectangle** body shape have bodies where their chest, waists and hips are all about the same width. Jackets with shoulder pads serve as a means of creating the illusion of a broader upper body but different focal points for the silhouette could just as easily include clothing items that accent the parts of the body that the man is most comfortable with.

Men with the **oval** body shape tend to have a large stomach and a generally round body. Avoiding shoulder pads in jackets and belts that are too thick or too narrow all aid in not adding the appearance of extra bulk. Additionally, well tailored, well fitting clothes are a must.

Men who have the **trapezoid** body shape have broad shoulders and chests with narrower waists and hips and, in general, they appear well proportioned. This body type in particular lends itself to experimentation in terms of colors, fabrics and different clothing silhouettes.

Building your wardrobe

Male clothing has a timeless versatility about it. This isn't to say that it's boring or that it hasn't been changed, but rather to illuminate the fact that a man in his 20s and a man in his 50s can own the exact same pieces and that neither of them will look out of place. Any man, anywhere could take the same 20 pieces and be well dressed almost anywhere in the world.

1. A black tuxedo A black tuxedo offers a perfect go-to outfit for almost every occasion requiring formal wear. Additionally, as there are a variety of menswear designers who have produced this piece, it is possible to find one that is flattering to any body shape and/or personality.

2. A white tuxedo shirt While such a white tuxedo shirt may not be consistently worn, it pairs effortlessly with a tuxedo for a look that is instantly put together.

3. Black dress shoes Black dress shoes go well with almost everything in the male wardrobe. Consider they can be paired with a tuxedo, a suit or slacks and a dress shirt.

4. A navy blue/black suit A navy blue suit conveys an air of assertiveness without being funeral in nature. Note that while a two piece suit (slacks and a jacket) is fine, and that a three piece suit (slacks, a jacket and a vest) offers more styling options. A black suit is also a great option in many situations.

5. A white dress shirt A crisp white dress shirt can be worn with almost anything else in the male wardrobe without looking out of place.

6. A light blue dress shirt A light blue dress shirt plays a similar role to the white dress shirt since it is also able to be worn with a variety of other pieces, but it offers a fresh pop of color.

7. A white/black tee shirt While it's an incredibly casual piece, a white tee shirt is also a very necessary piece and, as such, it should be as well fitting and well tailored as anything else in the male wardrobe. A black tee shirt is both casual and chic. Similar to the white tee shirt it should be well fitting and well tailored.

8. A lightweight cashmere sweater A lightweight cashmere sweater is a great layering piece that can be worn over your white tee in a casual setting, or over your white dress shirt in a more formal setting.

9. Medium or dark wash blue jeans Blue jeans are the ultimate in comfortable clothing and every man should have at least one pair in their wardrobe that's well tailored and a medium or dark wash.

10. Gray slacks Gray slacks offer men a more relaxed option to a suit when paired with a white dress shirt.

11. Black sneakers or driving shoes Shoes that are comfortable and casual can also look amazing. Black sneakers or driving shoes offer a more relaxed option for a man when he's wearing his jeans.

12. Burberry trench coat The Burberry trench coat is an iconic piece that is a must for any man. It adds a bit of elegance and sophistication to their wardrobes without being fussy.

13. Sandals A man may not immediately realize his need for a great pair of sandals, but they're a necessary investment for any man who'll be spending any time poolside or on the beach.

14. Linen pants Linen pants in a neutral color such as beige, white or grey offer an option for those who are vacationing and in need of something lighter in his wardrobe.

15. White short sleeved shirt A white short-sleeved shirt offers the perfect medium between a tee shirt and a dress shirt. Whether it's a polo or a button-down is the preference of the wearer and either way it's a great part of a more sophisticated spring/summer look.

16. A navy sport coat A navy sport coat can be paired with jeans for a more casual date, or worn with a pair of slacks to work.

17. Black leather jacket or wool pea coat A black leather jacket or wool pea coat serves as a perfect casual jacket in fall/early winter.

18. A "Power" tie While the man in your life may have a variety of ties, a red one is a must. It adds an immediate pop of strong color to any outfit.

19. A black leather belt While it's certainly more of an accessory; a black leather belt is an absolute must for any man as it will likely be one of the most worn pieces in his wardrobe. If possible, attempt to find one that's reversible and black on one side and brown on the other.

20. Dress socks Specific dress socks to be worn with suits are a must. Basic blacks or browns are okay, while argyle patterns offer a bit of extra style.

Just like the ladies, men are entitled to their own version of something special that speaks to them and shows off a bit of their personality. Below are five statement options for men.

1. **Aviators** Aviators are a classic accessory for men and never go out of style.

2. **Pocket Squares** By adding a pocket square to your suit you can add an immediate pop of color.

3. **A Timepiece** A timepiece, whether it's a sports watch or a Rolex, adds an immediate sense of style and sophistication to a man's look.

4. **Drivers** Drivers in a bold color, such as emerald green or orange, are great paired with denim or shorts.

5. **Cuff Links** Cuff links add a touch of elegance to any suit and can create a more polished look.

Basic Grooming

The basic grooming routine for men is much the same as it is for women in the sense that the focus should be on the hair, the skin and the nails.

Keep in mind that hair care for men can encompass both caring for the hair on their heads and manscaping the hair on their bodies. The former is a necessity, while the latter is a personal choice. The man in your life will likely have a barber that he already goes to, someone that he trusts to cut and trim his hair. This barber may also take care of his facial hair.

Skincare for men may seem much simpler than it is for women but that simply isn't the case. Even though they don't have to worry about leaving make-up on over night, it's become a lot more acceptable to them to get facials and to be aware of their skincare. Keep in mind, that just like women, they should have separate cleansers and moisturizers for their face and body, and should always wear sunscreen.

In terms of nail care, the man in your life should be cutting both his finger and toe nails on a regular basis, and if he's up for it, a manicure and/or pedicure can keep his nails looking neat and trim.

Keep in mind that consulting and working with professionals are a great way to help a man boost his confidence and his style. As an example of this with the help of a stylist, this basic wardrobe can be bolstered to capture the individual personality of any man to ensure that he both looks and feels his best.

Resources

"Fashion is very important. It is life enhancing and like everything that gives pleasure, it is worth doing well."- Vivienne Westwood

It's not always enough to know what to do, sometimes it helps to have some insight about where to go and what's so great about it. This portion of the book will give you some insight into the sources that I love and I hope you love them as well. For ease of readability they're segmented by chapter.

Please continue onto the next page to review the resources I have compiled.

Chapter 2

There are some amazing designers and websites that cater specifically to plus-size, petite and tall women, and here are just a few of them. Keep in mind that while there aren't many sites that cater specifically to a petite client base that there are many well known stores and brands that have pieces available for this group, just make sure that they based their sizing on height.

Plus-size

The site: http://www.igigi.com/

Why I love it: The selection of items on this site is amazing and they have everything from on-trend day wear to bridal gowns.

Recommendations: Check out the "limited collection" which features pieces that are perfect for whatever the current season is.

The site: http://www.swakdesigns.com/

Why I love it: It's one of the few places I've come across, online or off, that provide vintage-inspired pieces for plus sized-women that look fashion forward and wearable.

Recommendations: Check out the "Curvy Kitten" section of the website which is the one that offers the retro looking pieces

The site: http://qristylfrazierdesigns.com/

Why I love it: The site shows that plus-size can be sexy with pieces that are figure flattering and unabashedly bold.

Recommendations: There are a couple of collections available at any time, take the time to look at them all.

Petite

The site: http://the16thbar.com/shop/

Why I love it: The 16th bar represents one of the few exclusively plus-size lines that's available in the United States and the pieces are fashion forward without being dated.

Recommendations: Follow the blog of the site to get a better feel for the line and what may be released in the future.

Tall

The site: http://us.longtallsally.com/?gclid=CK6xh4-J67YCFUyY4AodbzwA4g

Why I love it: The site offers a wide range of pieces at prices that allow you to experiment with various colors and patterns.

Recommendations: If you prefer the option of perusing the clothes offline, take advantage of the option to request a catalog.

The site: http://www.heightgoddess.com/

Why I love it: The site offers a great mix of basic and statements pieces and is the perfect stop for a tall woman who wants a mix of timeless and trendy pieces. Plus, they spotlight women who are making a difference.

Recommendations: Don't keep the site and its goodies to yourself. Splurge on a few e-gift cards for your tall friends.

The site: http://www.simplytall.net/

Why I love it: The company is family owned and operated, and their selection is constantly expanding.

Recommendations: Take advantage of the ability to shop for pants and leggings by inseam.

Chapter 3

Building your capsule collection begins with making sure that you have the right foundation garments. Here are a few places to go before you go anywhere else.

The site: http://senselingerie.com/D-Up-Cups-Freedom-Bra-P895C26.aspx

Why I love it: With plunging backs and other backless looks being a great look, it's nice to be able to offer that option to women with larger breasts.

Recommendations: If you're only going to purchase one of these, be sure to purchase it in beige which is the most neutral color available.

The site: http://www.myintimacy.com/

Why I love it: Considering that many women aren't wearing the correct size bra, I adore a site that seeks to help rectify that.

Recommendations: While there are limited sites that offer bra fitting, I strongly suggest that if there's one near you that you make a reservation.

Chapter 5

It would be impossible for me to tell you all of the stores that I love for both my own wardrobe and those of my clients; there are just so many incredible places.

E-boutiques

The site: http://www.my-wardrobe.com/

Why I love it: The option to "Shop by wardrobe" is an inspired one and a definite plus if you need to pick out a piece for a specific destination or occasion, and don't want to have to sift through pieces that may be inappropriate.

Recommendations: Take full advantage of how well laid out this site is. Links like "New in" and "Trends" are particularly tempting, in addition to the aforementioned "Shop by wardrobe" function.

The site: http://www.modewalk.com/

Why I love it: The site is both clean and easy to navigate. Additionally, there's a "Meet the designer" feature under each item which provides a bit of biography on who created the piece.

Recommendations: When advice such as "item runs small" is given be sure to take it. Also, be sure to consult the size chart for any designers you aren't familiar with.

The site: http://www.lespommettes.com/index.php

Why I love it: Les Pommmettes does not sell any pieces which include leather, suede, skins, bones, teeth, claws, ivory or feathers. This is amazing for vegetarian and vegan women who want amazing pieces and moreover want to know that what they're purchasing is in line with what they believe.

Recommendations: Don't be afraid of the "view all" buttons. Unlike a lot of other sites, the layout stays super clean and easy to follow even with this feature implemented.

The site: http://www.kirnazabete.com/

Why I love it: The site features a great mix of designers I adore such as Alexander Wang, Lanvin and Giambattista Valli. Also, once you're on a designer page, you can see exactly how many pieces come in a particular size and narrow your search based on that.

Recommendations: On each designer page there's a link that shows other designers you may like. This is a great way to find designers with similar aesthetics to the lines you already like.

The site: http://www.farfetch.com

Why I love it: This site offers access to boutiques in both North America and Europe which is a rare find.

Recommendations: Go to the "Boutiques" link and click on where you're interested in shopping. You'll be treated to an incredibly detailed list of the boutiques in that area including where they're located, when they were established, brands to look out for and a link to shop.

The site: http://www.shoplesnouvelles.com/

Why I love it: Visually the site is beautiful, navigation is a dream and there's an amazing mix of designers including Elizabeth and James and 3.1. Phillip Lim.

Recommendations: Sign up for the style news and updates to keep abreast of what's coming soon as all designers aren't available at all times.

The site: http://freshionable.com/freshionable-blog/

Why I love it: The site offers super fashionable pieces picked out especially for fashion forward professionals and are created by emerging designers.

Recommendations: Check out the "Designers" section which showcases interviews with the emerging talent featured on the site and take advantage of the "Shop" which allows users to hone in on a wide array of potential preferences.

The site: http://www.net-a-porter.com/

Why I love it: The site is well laid out, easy to navigate and offers an amazing selection of pieces from high-end designers with amazing aesthetics like Alexander McQueen, Marchesa and Jil Sander, showcasing all aspects of their collections and not simply clothing.

Recommendations: When you're viewing the site by designer there's an option to sign up for updates of the designer you're looking at. Doing that will help you keep abreast of new pieces.

International e-boutiques

The site: http://www.mytheresa.com/us_en/

Why I love it: Aside from exclusive partnerships with Balenciaga and Tod's, the site offers up new arrivals three times a week (Monday, Wednesday and Friday) and has 1-4 day flat rate shipping which includes custom duties and processing fees.

Recommendations: Visit the site when you have some time to really look around and appreciate all of the amazing pieces that they offer. Additionally, be sure to check the size and fit information provided for each piece.

The site: http://www.montaignemarket.com/index_EN.html

Why I love it: Montaigne Market was the first multibrand and shop on avenue Montaigne in Paris and, as such, they feature a wide array of designers including personal favorites of mine Missoni, Saint Laurent Paris and Isabel Marant

Recommendations: When orderingm make sure you have Euros on hand as you have to pay the import fees upon delivery.

The site: http://www.notjustalabel.com/

Why I love it: The site exists as a portal for emerging designers from around the world to sell their creations and the offerings are an amazing mix of pieces.

Recommendations: If you have any questions at all about your order or are feeling a bit hesitant about something, email their customer support team.

The site: http://www.vestiairecollective.com/

Why I love it: This site is like one giant treasure hunt. Rather than acting as a traditional boutique, it's a luxury resale market boasting authentic pieces from amazing designers like Miu Miu and Reed Krakoff.

Recommendations: If you're looking for something by a particular designer, utilize the "Create an alert" feature which will update you when new pieces are available.

The site: http://www.lindelepalais.com/en-US

Why I love it: In addition to being a beautifully designed site with a wide array of offerings, the site also includes the cost of shipping for items sent to the United States. As a bonus, scrolling over any item will let you know the sizes that it's currently available in, allowing you to browse without constantly clicking if the pieces you're interested in aren't in your size.

Recommendations: Utilize the "Guide" feature that appears when you click on a piece as it will handle the size conversion for you.

The site: http://www.luisaviaroma.com/home.aspx?userlang=EN

Why I love it: The site features an amazing mix of well-known designers and feature their pieces alongside those of up-and-coming fashion talents.

Recommendations: Go to the designer list, which is incredibly well organized, and take the time to check out some of those listed under the "New Talents" section and find yourself pleasantly surprised.

The site: http://www.forzieri.com/usa/Default.asp?l=usa&c=usa

Why I love it: The focus of this site is Italian and European brands like personal favorites Valentino and Vivienne Westwood. Plus, with express delivery, you can have your order in 1-2 business days and their standard delivery only takes 4-5 days.

Recommendations: Check out their "Travel and Business" section before you checkout for some great pieces, such as briefcases and baby garment bags.

The site: http://myasho.com/Welcome

Why I love it: Africa isn't immediately thought of as a fashion mecca, but there are some amazing pieces that come from this continent and the site shows them off.

Recommendations: Be sure to check out the "Couture" section as well as the jackets and dresses.

The site: http://watch-that-label.com/

Why I love it: The entire site is dedicated to high-end emerging fashion talents and offers up pieces, some of which have been seen in magazines like Vogue and Elle.

Recommendations: Check out the "Meet the designer" feature. If the designer isn't currently available you can sign up for an email alert. If the designer does have pieces available, you can check out the key designs or shop the full collection.

The site: http://www.shopthemag.com/

Why I love it: The site features Asia's top fashion names, designers which may not be immediately recognized in the United States but who craft some amazing pieces.

Recommendations: Since the designers may not immediately be familiar to you, dive right in and look at all of the clothes at once. Also pay close attention to the "size and fit" guidelines offered with each piece.

Customized and Limited edition

The site: http://www.seambliss.com/

Why I love it: As a customer, the site lets you create a client account and from there you can post a project to have something designed to your exact specifications.

Recommendations: To get a feel for the work of some of the designers on the site and what they may be capable of producing check out the "Shop" section.

The site: http://www.shoesofprey.com/

Why I love it: The site allows users the option to create a pair of completely customized shoes. There are 12 shoe shapes, over a 100 colors and each pair is handmade.

Recommendations: The site allows users a number of appealing options, including the ability to take an "it" color or shoe shape and construct a shoe that's on trend but also unique. It's also a great way to build your shoe collection or create basic or statement footwear pieces that truly capture your style and personality.

The site: http://www.milkandhoneyshoes.com/

Why I love it: In addition to 12 different shoe shapes and 14 different types of materials, the site also offers numerous strap and embellishment options for a pair that's your perfect fit. Additionally, on select styles they can go as low as a 31 and as high as a 44.

Recommendations: For silk shoes in particular, keep in mind that the company will send you swatches which will be an amazing help if you're looking to match something in particular.

The site: http://www.trendseeder.com/

Why I love it: The site offers exclusive pieces from emerging designers and works in limited quantities, meaning it's highly unlikely that you'll end up somewhere in the exact same piece as someone else when you shop this site.

Recommendations: The collections are generally very small so take the time to check out everything.

The site: http://www.ariella.com/

Why I love it: The site features beautiful cocktail and evening dresses and every piece in the Ariella Couture collection is a limited edition.

Recommendations: Note that the pieces are listed in UK sizes so check out the size and fit guide for proper conversions, and if you have any questions email them to inquiry before ordering.

The site: http://ofakind.com/

Why I love it: The site features limited edition accessories, apparel and jewelry. Each of the designers is hand-selected and any pieces on the site are exclusive.

Recommendations: Utilize the option to hide the sold out pieces.

The site: http://www.20ltd.com/

Why I love it: This super sleek site features luxury pieces in very limited quantities and as such every piece is something amazing.

Recommendations: Go for the fashion options but look around at what else they have to offer.

The site: http://www.eshakti.com/default.aspx

Why I love it: The range of sizes on this site is incredible going from 0-36w and each piece can be left as shown or altered to add or remove length, adjust the neckline and alter sleeves for a final piece that suits you and your body.

Recommendations: Opt for the custom sizing which allows you to input your exact measurements for the best fit possible.

Members only

The site: http://modaoperandi.com/

Why I love it: The site provides members with daily updates on which designer trunk shows are live, which ones are ending and which ones are coming soon.

Recommendations: Keep in mind that any item you order from a trunk show is a pre-order and not immediately ready for shipment. If you're looking for a bit of instant gratification while you're waiting, be sure to check out the boutique which features items that are available now.

The site: http://www.shopittome.com/

Why I love it: The site allows you to personalize what items it'll alert you of by letting you select what sizes you're interested in and what designers you favor, helping to create completely personalized emails letting you know when pieces are available and more importantly where you can get them.

Recommendations: You can select whether you want alerts daily, weekly or twice a week, so be sure to select something that works with your schedule. Also keep in mind that you can take a break from notices without losing your membership, which is great if you have a period of time where you don't plan on checking your email.

The site: http://www.gilt.com/

Why I love it: The site offers flash sales from great designers such as Oscar De La Renta, Tom Ford and Missoni.

Recommendations: Take the time to preview the sales when the option is made available. That'll give you some insight into whether or not it'll be worth shopping for you.

The site: http://www.ruelala.com/

Why I love it: The site offers pieces from an amazing array of designers such as Proenza Schouler and it's flash sale format means that you can hone in on what you want.

Recommendations: Take full advantage of the "Still want it" and "reminder" features. With the former, if something sells out before the sale fully ends there may still be a way to get it, just click the quantity you want and provide your billing and shipping info, if they can get it to you they will. With the latter feature you can see the overview of sales a few days in advance and set email reminders for anything that interests you.

The site: https://www.niftythrifty.com/Collections/Home.sls

Why I love it: While not a haven for high-end designers, the site is still a shoppers dream with beautifully curated collections available in flash sales that last for a few days.

Recommendations: Explore the site over the course of a few days or a week. Chances are good that you'll find a few pieces that'll inspire you to buy.

The site: https://www.vaunte.com/

Why I love it: Imagine a consignment shop where all of the pieces came from people like designers, buyers and fashion marketing directors and you have Vaunte.

Recommendations: After signing up you can shop by designer or size, this will allow you to better focus on the pieces rather than the personalities behind them.

The site: https://www.opensky.com/home

Why I love it: Opensky is sort of like Facebook if everyone you followed was an expert in their field and selling something you might genuinely be interested in.

Recommendations: Limit your scope. The site isn't solely limited to fashion and so it's very easy to fill your feed with a whole array of interests, just keep in mind the stuff you're really intrigued by.

The site: http://www.fadmashion.com/

Why I love it: The site solely focuses on emerging New York based designers and acts as both a collective and boutique.

Recommendations: While membership isn't mandatory to shop the site, there are some perks that come with joining such as exclusive pricing and the ability to share and save your favorites.

Consignment

The site: http://www.myhautecloset.com/

Why I love it: This is an online consignment shop that deals specifically in high-end pieces. Plus, every piece is guaranteed authentic.

Recommendations: If you're unsure how you feel about the idea of purchasing pre-owned pieces, browsing this site is a good way to get a feel for the concept from the comfort of your own space.

The site: http://refashioner.com/

Why I love it: The site isn't just a boutique, it can also become a way for you to get rid of some of your older or less loved pieces if you're open to the community aspect of it all. Keep in mind that while you become a member at checkout that you don't have to do anything but shop.

Recommendations: Truly get into the spirit of the site and look through your own closet. Is there anything you don't wear or don't love that someone else might?

Chapter 6

Great shoes and standout accessories are a fundamental part of any wardrobe, and as such, it's important to know that there are places that offer these items exclusively.

Shoes

The site: http://www.shoptheshoebox.com/

Why I love it: The Shoe Box has brick and mortar locations in both New York and Boca Raton which makes it accessible Offline as well as Online, plus it offers shoes from designers like Vince Camuto, Chloe and Stuart Weitzman.

Recommendations: Be sure to check out both the "New arrivals" and "exclusive" sections.

The site:
http://www.barefoottess.com/?AID=10597942&PID=1157687

Why I love it: This site solely sells shoes in sizes 10-15 which is perfect for taller women who may require larger shoes and still want to look fashionable. Plus the site offers special sizing including both narrow and wide fit.

Recommendations: Utilize the "shop by size" feature so that you can filter out shoes available in your size only.

The site: http://www.jildorshoes.com/

Why I love it: This site carries an amazing array of sizes, including shoes with both narrow and wide widths and has a long list of designers.

Recommendations: Resist the urge to shop by category or designer and choose instead to shop by size. This way you'll only see what's available that will fit you in case you decide to buy. Also note that once you've activated that feature that you can then narrow your search further, selecting things like desired heel height, style or color.

The site: https://www.emylooshoes.com/

Why I love it: The site offers shoes as small as a US3 and has a great selection of shoes that are made for women as opposed to for kids, which is perfect for petite women who may also have smaller feet.

Recommendations: Utilize the size chart to learn how to measure your feet.

The site: http://www.heels.com/

Why I love it: As a site solely dedicated to shoes, the site has an amazing selection. Additionally, most items ship via UPS free of charge and are available in two days.

Recommendations: Check out the "Fashionality" feature as a way to search after narrowing the selection down by size. You may find some shoes that are perfect that you never would have picked out if you chose to search another way.

The site: http://www.shoescribe.com/

Why I love it: This is a site for true shoe lovers. Some of their stellar features include an order library, which is a complete history of every pair you order and which allows you to print off labels to help organize your shoe collection and, if you join, you also get customized alerts when pieces matching your taste become available.

Recommendations: Check out the "Spotlight" link for a series of curated collections.

The site: http://www.dianaekelly.com/

Why I love it: I adore the "Flats for philanthropy" program in which 10% of the proceeds from a specially chosen or designed pair of flats goes to a pre-selected charity.

Recommendations: Take your time and truly peruse the site. The selection is more limited than what you'll find on other sites and every collection is worth looking at.

The site: http://shop.tabithasimmons.com/

Why I love it: Tabitha Simmons makes shoes that are chic and sophisticated. Plus, while what she produces fits with the trends. There's also something timeless about her pieces as well.

Recommendations: Her collections are fairly small so be sure to look around. Also, if something is out of stock in your size online, check the store list and see if there's someplace nearby that can help you.

The site: http://www.tiltedsole.com/

Why I love it: Sometimes our shoes need to be the undisputed stars of the show and this site is full of shoes that fit that bill. It's certainly not something for everyone, but if you're into bold shoes like those by Betsey Johnson or Jeffrey Campbell then you'll love this site.

Recommendations: Even if you're not sure how you feel about incredibly bold footwear spend a few minutes on the site. You may surprise yourself.

The site: http://www.beyondskin.co.uk/

Why I love it: While I'm not personally a vegetarian or vegan, I appreciate the desire of the women who are who want shoes that are amazing and still in line with their morals.

Recommendations: Keep in mind that the prices on the site aren't USD and that the site itself doesn't convert the pricing so it will change based on the strength of the dollar.

Accessories

The site: http://boticca.com/

Why I love it: Boticca features some incredible emerging talent from around the world all in one place. Plus, every piece has a story.

Recommendations: Sign up for the site so you can utilize unique features like the ability to contact the designers directly.

The site: http://www.ahalife.com

Why I love it: The site is well organized, easy to navigate and full of amazing pieces that are interesting and beautifully crafted.

Recommendations: Succumb to the urge to look at the other offerings. While the site has beautiful jewelry and accessories, it really is about building a lifestyle so let your eyes wander to some of their other categories as well.

The site: http://www.warbyparker.com/

Why I love it: The eyewear featured on this site is sleek and chic. Plus, there's a philanthropic aspect that means every time someone buys a pair of glasses, a pair is donated to someone in need.

Recommendations: If there isn't a showroom near you, utilize their virtual try on feature which lets you upload a picture and use that image as your model.

The site: http://www.brilliantearth.com/

Why I love it: Diamonds may be a girls' best friend but the ways in which they sometimes get to us are a bit disturbing, which is why I adore the fact that this company only uses conflict-free stones.

Recommendations: The feature to build your own ring is great if you're looking for something that's completely suited to your taste so I definitely suggest trying it.

The site: http://www.sadeesays.com/shop/

Why I love it: This site features fashion jewelry at its most current, which means it's a must shop if you're looking for pieces that are trendy.

Recommendations: Check out the "Trends" section for pieces that are perfect for the current season and may become your signature if you carry them into the next.

The site: http://arturorios.com/

Why I love it: Hats often don't get enough credit for the additions that they can make to a look. Arturo Rios provides true statement pieces that are equally whimsical and wearable.

Recommendations: Even if you're not getting married, check out the bridal collection for hats and fascinators in a range of white a neutral tones that are incredibly feminine.

The site: http://www.brahmin.com/

Why I love it: Their pieces are stylish and their collections are incredibly cohesive. Plus, in addition to bags, they also create a wide array of accessories such as contact cases and tablet cases.

Recommendations: Be sure to check out the "Web exclusives" for pieces that are only available Online.

The site: http://www.lodis.com/home-page

Why I love it: In addition to beautiful bags and wallets, LODIS also offers brilliant belts which can be just the thing to pull together an outfit both literally and figuratively.

Recommendations: Be sure to check out the accessories section which includes some great pieces like business card and credit card cases.

The site: http://www.lineapelle.com/

Why I love it: Linea Pelle specializes in casual luxury, so while the pieces are stylish they're also capable of being staples in your wardrobe.

Recommendations: Check out the monogram feature which will let you add up to three initials to select bags helping to make the piece uniquely yours.

The site: http://www.monamoore.com/

Why I love it: One word: Vintage. There's an entire section on this site dedicated to vintage accessories from designers like Chanel and YSL.

Recommendations: Check out the "Accessories" section which features items such as scarves and gloves, which can help add instant drama to a look. Also, be sure to look at what vintage pieces are available.

Chapter 7

Knowing what to splurge on and where and how to save is one of the things that separates true fashionistas from the casual shopper. Making such distinctions isn't always easy though and so it helps to have a bit of guidance from someone who knows where to look and what you're likely to find.

The site: https://www.everlane.com/

Why I love it: The site features luxury pieces like silk blouses in both classic and contemporary colors for incredibly reasonable prices.

Recommendations: Don't solely stock up on your basics, the site features a men's section as well so you'll be able to purchase pieces for your dad, brother, boyfriend, husband or male best friend as well.

The site: http://www.renttherunway.com

Why I love it: With a stock that's frequently updated, the site offers rentals for pieces that are fashion forward and with a focus on more formal events, it's the perfect answer of what to wear for everything from New Year's Eve to the wedding of a friend.

Recommendations: Take advantage of both the detailed size information and the option to order the same dress in multiple sizes to ensure your best chance for a fabulous fit.

The site: http://www.bagborroworsteal.com/

Why I love it: There are certain bags that are amazing for a season but simply not something that you'd put into regular rotation in your wardrobe for whatever reason. Additionally, the site lets you try out different styles of bags which can be helpful in picking out bags to buy.

Recommendations: Be sure to check out the "New Arrivals" section if you're interested in pieces that are especially trendy, since these will be the most current pieces available and as such definitely in season.

The site: http://www.emitations.com/

Why I love it: Sometimes you see something on the red carpet that you know would look amazing in your collection, and considering that those pieces are often borrowed, why not buy something incredibly similar for a fraction of the cost and none of the worry if it gets misplaced.

Recommendations: Each category on the site has a great deal of subcategories, truly take the time to look at each to ensure that you're truly seeing all that they have to offer.

Chapter 10

Looking good goes a long way in helping to ensure that you feel good. This means not only making sure that your clothes are fabulous, but also on taking good care of your hair skin and nails, as well as regularly taking time to do a little extra and pamper yourself.

The site: http://www.plasticsurgery.org/

Why I love it: Plastic surgery isn't for everyone, but everyone should know where to go to find a plastic surgeon that's board certified should the need or desire arise.

Recommendations: If you're considering reconstructive or cosmetic plastic surgery then go to the "Find a surgeon" link on the site and locate one in your area to perform the procedure.

Chapter 11

Men's fashion is absolutely amazing and while there are plenty of places to purchase basics from, there are also numerous places to find trendier pieces. Brick-and-mortar stores offer a more tactile experience but e-tailers are accessible to everyone.

The site: http://www.oki-ni.com/

Why I love it: The site offers an amazing mix of well-known brands for both clothing and footwear as well as a great mix of casual and semi-formal pieces.

Recommendations: The default pricing on the website isn't USD so make sure that you change this before proceeding so that you know exactly what you're going to be spending.

The site: http://www.mrporter.com/

Why I love it: The site really is about more than just clothes, it's about helping men to cultivate a lifestyle that's stylish, fashion forward and still fully their own which I appreciate.

Recommendations: Check out the "What's new" section for the pieces that are particularly on trend, and also check out "The journal" which is an online magazine of sorts that's updated on a weekly basis. As a bonus it's possible to shop just for the items featured in this section.

The site: http://biasedcut.com/shirts-splash/

Why I love it: As much as I love both retailers and e-tailers that offer a variety, I'm also enamored by those that do just one or two things provided, and they do them exceptionally well. And this site is an amazing example of the latter and offers nothing but shirts.

Recommendations: Engage the help of a stylist to aid with getting the most accurate measurements possible. Each shirt is custom sewn so it's especially important that the measurements you provide are accurate. Also, don't expect the shirts to be delivered in less than two weeks specifically because they're tailor-made.

The site: http://www.sneakoutfitters.com/

Why I love it: Express shipping in the U.S. can be completed in as few as 2 days, which is amazing if you're seeking out more immediate gratification from an online shopping experience. Plus, the site also features sample sales which you can check out if you're in New York.

Recommendations: Take advantage of the lower price point offered by this site for a chance to stock up on some pieces for the man or men in your life who are looking to add some more fashion forward pieces into their wardrobes. As a bonus, because a lot of the pieces are slim fit, they can also be utilized to add some interesting pieces to your own closets if you're opting for a boyfriend look that isn't overly boxy.

The site: http://sg.burberry.com/store/bespoke/

Why I love it: The Burberry trench coat is an iconic piece and this site allows you the chance to create one that meets your specifications, including but not limited to the ability to alter length, select from several classic colors and even add a monogram if you choose to do so.

Recommendations: After creating one of these coats for the man in your life, create one for yourself as they have options for women as well.

The site: http://www.allenedmonds.com/

Why I love it: This site is a great destination for mens footwear that ranges from casual to classic dress with colors that are both basic and bold.

Recommendations: Take advantage of the ability to shop for shoes by color as opposed to by style, this will show you some options in hues that you're looking for and may open your eyes to a style that you wouldn't have considered before.

The site: http://www.lyonstate.com/

Why I love it: This site has an incredibly clean and inviting design which matches the preppier clothes that they sell. Keep in mind that while the pieces are definitely more classic than trendy that they're perfect for building a wardrobe.

Recommendations: Check out the in-house collection Lyonsate which features hand tailored shirts all made in the U.S.

Ashley's Glam Squad

Sara Fischer
Makeup Artist/ Owner
Real Beauty Makeup Artistry
www.RealBeautyPB.com
Sara@RealBeautyPB.com

Jeremy Carta
Hair Artist
Janthonycarta@Gmail.com
Bio on www.JulienFarel.com under 5th Avenue salon
(786) 431-6774

Emily Peterson
CEO/Aesthetician
SkinRxMd Skincare
www.Skinrxmd.com
(561) 999-5559

Andra Hernett-Taksey
Boca Brows
Eyebrow Specialist/Owner
Andra@BocaBrows.com
(561) 370-9482

I'd love to hear more from you and learn all about your styling needs!

http://www.AshleyMartini.com/

On Facebook: https://www.facebook.com/MartiniFashions

On Linkedin: http://www.linkedin.com/in/ashleymartini

On Instagram check out "MartiniFashionsLLC"

On Twitter follow @MartiniFashions

COMMIT TO LOOKING
YOUR BEST TODAY!

The benefit to working with a personal stylist is to maximize the impact of your wardrobe and add to your confidence level.

Call or E-Mail me Today! 1-(914) 204-4198 | AM@AshleyMartini.com
or visit: www.AshleyMartini.com

The following are just some of the services that I can provide for you.

- **Fit Session** – A fit session involves a personalized assessment of both your body type and what will be most flattering on you.

- **Closet Consultation and Makeover** – I provide closet consultations, and makeovers utilizing my exclusive ASSERT closet organization process, while taking into account the comfort level of the client.

- **Personal Makeover** – In partnering with various salons and beauty/health service providers, I am able to facilitate clients who are seeking to find or refine a complete look.

- **Personal Shopping** – I will either provide a one-on-one shopping session or shop on my clients' behalf with specific client needs and requests in mind.

- **Bridal Styling** – This includes engagement photo styling, wedding dress shopping, groom's attire selection, bridal boudoir image styling, bridal party dress selection, and honey moon shopping

- **Event Styling** – By combining my personal shopping and makeover services it is possible for me to help transform you for the special events in your life

- **Men's Styling** – I provide all of my services for men, as well as ladies.

- **Maternity Styling** – Being pregnant does not mean having to give up style for 9 months. I am available for personal shopping and fit sessions for each trimester of your pregnancy to help ensure that you can be chic and confident during this time.

- **Children's Styling (newborn – 12 years old)** – I understand the needs of parents who want their children to be well dressed. I am available for closet consultations and modified personal shopping sessions for your children.

- **Teenage Styling (13 years old – 18 years old)** – I am available for both closet consultations and modified personal shopping sessions for your teenagers.

- **Editorial** – I am available for both commercial and fashion styling.